A ***Promise*** *to all* GENERATIONS

STORIES & ESSAYS ABOUT *Social Security* & *Frances Perkins*

EDITED BY

CHRISTOPHER
BREISETH AND
KIRSTIN DOWNEY

THE FRANCES PERKINS CENTER
NEWCASTLE, MAINE

The Frances Perkins Center, Newcastle, Maine 04553
FrancesPerkinsCenter.org
© 2011 The Frances Perkins Center
All rights reserved

Art on the cover and throughout the book is from a mural titled "The Meaning of
Social Security" by Ben Shahn, painted in 1940–1942 in the lobby of the building
that formerly housed the Social Security Administration, now the home
of the Voice of America, in Washington, D.C.

Photography: Chris Eichler
Book design: Harrah Lord, Yellow House Studio
Copyeditor: Elizabeth IlgenFritz

Printed in the United States of America
ISBN: 978-0-615-41722-6
Library of Congress Control Number: 2010940288
First Edition

The people are what matter to government,
and a government should aim to give all the people under
its jurisdiction the best possible life.

———

FRANCES PERKINS

Contents

_____

Foreword

———

TOMLIN PERKINS COGGESHALL

As Frances Perkins's only grandchild, Tomlin Coggeshall remembers his grandmother as a warm, loving person who took him toy shopping at FAO Schwartz and introduced him to train conductors and engineers at Grand Central Station. He is the original founder of the Frances Perkins Center and serves on its board of directors. An expert in hydrogen energy and alternative fuels, he still resides in an 1837 Maine brick farmhouse built with bricks made in the family brickyard on land owned by his forebears since the mid-1700s.

THIS BOOK ON THE ROOTS OF SOCIAL SECURITY AND ITS IMPACT on America is a collection of essays from some of today's key thinkers on social insurance as well as personal stories from beneficiaries of Social Security. We are reminded that Social Security, as conceived of by my grandmother, Frances Perkins, and her colleagues, is a system of insurance whereby premiums are collected and benefits are paid out. It has never been a handout. In fact, President Franklin D. Roosevelt warned my grandmother in no uncertain terms when they were conceiving what they initially called an old age pension system, "Frances, I won't have the dole!"

She crafted a plan that was definitely not the dole. Their efforts created a national economic buffer that workers paid into until they or their families needed the benefits for one reason or another, including unemployment, disability, retirement, or death. The most common reason for receiving Social Security benefits is retirement. But what FDR referred to as "the vicissitudes of life" when he signed the Social Security Act into law on August 14, 1935, are also covered by this now vital social insurance system.

In the photo of the signing of the Act, you can see my grandmother standing directly behind FDR. Others whose wisdom and efforts helped create the program are close by, including Senator Robert Wagner of New York and Congressman John Dingell, Sr. of Michigan. We have them and their Congressional colleagues to thank for much of the economic security that has persisted even in these turbulent and unpredictable times. The crash of 2008 would have been much worse had we not had funds flowing to families of unemployed and retired people, allowing them to purchase their daily necessities and thus pump cash into their local economy.

My grandmother's roots in New England gave her a thrifty instinct. She understood the effect of boom and bust cycles on the lives of self-sufficient Americans. Indeed, my great-grandparents were forced to leave Maine when the family brickyard could no longer support them. While a student at Mount Holyoke College, my grandmother was introduced to the tenuous situation faced by New England factory workers—men, women, and children who had no economic security whatsoever. As she rose from her career as a social worker to her leadership role of the industrial commission of New York State under Governor Alfred E. Smith and Governor Franklin D. Roosevelt, and finally to her role as President Roosevelt's Secretary of Labor, she was constantly motivated by the desire to help the less fortunate. Considered the mother of Social Security, Frances Perkins is still helping each and every one of us prepare for our retirement and protect our loved ones in case of our demise or disablement. I invite you to browse our website (FrancesPerkinsCenter.org) to learn more about her amazing career and to watch and listen to her speak on videotapes and audiotapes.

The Frances Perkins Center was formed to honor my grandmother's accomplishments, to share the history of her life and career, and to carry forward her work for social justice. We are devoted to actively contributing to and affecting the debate over the safety net she helped create; supporting and strengthening Social Security is a top priority. My grandmother considered the program her most significant accomplishment. She strove to provide "the best possible life" for working men and women across the nation.

Acknowlegdments

———

BARBARA BURT

THIS PROJECT STARTED AS AN IDEA BATTED AROUND A TABLE at St. Andrews Church in Newcastle, Maine, in September of 2009. A group of friends, staff, and board members of the Frances Perkins Center had met to plan programs for the coming year. We knew that the 75th anniversary of Social Security would be our main focus; we were thinking about the best way to draw attention to the program that so many Americans, while relying upon it, also seemed to take for granted.

That sunny morning we had no idea that Social Security and the philosophy behind it would become major areas of contention once again. It's been a strange experience to discover that even after three-quarters of a century of transformative effectiveness, this government program still has enemies working for its demise. Thus, the project that began as an accolade was transformed into a vehicle for explaining and defending what Frances Perkins described as her most important accomplishment.

We are immensely grateful to the writers who have contributed their stories and essays to this collection, as well as to the many individuals who have shared their personal Social Security stories with us. As these personal narratives arrived via email, phone call, and letter, we were often brought to tears by the mixture of tragedy and hope they contained.

None of the writers was paid; all profits from the sale of this book go to the nonprofit Frances Perkins Center. We also thank the National Academy of Social Insurance for providing partial funding for the project. The book was carefully nurtured by its two editors, Christopher Breiseth and Kirstin Downey, whose vast knowledge of Frances Perkins and the New Deal contributed to the depth and breadth of the story told in these pages.

A Promise to All Generations is meant to commemorate and celebrate Social Security, to increase general knowledge and understanding of the program, and to provide analyses and strategies that can help those working to ensure the program's viability for the next 75 years and beyond. We hope you will find we've succeeded.

Barbara Burt is executive director of the Frances Perkins Center

President Roosevelt signs Social Security Act with Secretary Perkins looking on.
LIBRARY OF CONGRESS PHOTO, LC-US262-123278.

Frances Perkins in 1935

Introduction

CHRISTOPHER N. BREISETH

Christopher N. Breiseth was president and CEO of the Franklin and Eleanor Roosevelt Institute in Hyde Park, New York, from 2001 to 2009. He is president emeritus of Wilkes University which he served from 1984 to 2001. From 1960 to 1965, when he was completing his Ph.D. in history, he knew Frances Perkins because they both lived in the Telluride House at Cornell University, a relationship he described in "The Frances Perkins I Knew," written in 1966, the year after her death. Now retired, both he and his wife are Social Security and Medicare recipients as were all their parents, several of their siblings, and multiple aunts and uncles. Medicare has been particularly important in covering several very expensive illnesses of family members.

*T*he first time I met Frances Perkins was in the spring of 1960. My fellow students at the Telluride House at Cornell University had invited Miss Perkins, a Visiting Professor in the Industrial Labor and Relations School at Cornell, to join us for dinner and a talk afterwards.[1] To get the questioning going after dinner, I asked her what she regarded as her most important contribution. She answered in two words: "Social Security."

This volume celebrates the 75th anniversary of Social Security, arguably the most important legacy of Franklin Roosevelt's New Deal. It presents the voices of everyday Americans whose lives and whose families' lives have been profoundly influenced by this comprehensive social insurance program. The Social Security legislation, signed by President Roosevelt on August 14, 1935, included in addition to old age retirement pensions, unemployment insurance and widows' and surviving children's benefits. Subsequent amendments provided support for dependent children and for workers who become disabled and their families.

Also included in this volume are thirteen essays from authorities on different aspects of Social Security—its development, the struggle over its passage, its implementation, its impact on America and Americans, and the battle that is being waged now over its future. Pivotal to this story is the central role of Frances Perkins, FDR's Secretary of Labor, the first female cabinet member in U.S. history, who accepted this position only after extracting from President-elect Roosevelt a promise to support her in adopting an old age insurance program.

ADAM COHEN, author of *Nothing to Fear: FDR's Inner Circle and the Hundred Days that Created Modern America*, in the first essay, paints a portrait of what America was like before the New Deal when there was virtually no governmental support for people in their old age. Studies in several states in the 1920s and early 1930s showed that nearly half the residents over 65 did not have subsistence incomes. With the Great Depression, Cohen observes, destitution "was no longer hidden out of sight, on the other side of the tracks or in the inner-city slums." The first two and a half years of the Roosevelt Administration's active response to the Depression, plus growing public pressure to deal with the misery of the elderly, paved the way for Social Security in August of 1935. Cohen demonstrates the central importance of Frances Perkins in partnering with FDR to win Congress's support for Social Security.

KARENNA GORE SCHIFF featured Frances Perkins in her book, *Lighting the Way: Nine Women Who Changed Modern America*. In the second essay in this book, Schiff shows how Miss Perkins came of age as part of a network of women social workers that was pressing a progressive political agenda to ameliorate the appalling working conditions of women and children. Inspired by and working with the likes of Florence Kelley and Jane Addams, Frances Perkins moved from hands-on social work in Chicago, Philadelphia, and New York, pursuing graduate education in sociology, economics, and political science at the University of Pennsylvania and Columbia University along the way, to engage directly with politicians—especially Thomas McManus of Tammany Hall in New York State—to gain support for reforms addressing the conditions of labor and factory safety. Based on her work to secure precedent-setting fire safety regulations in the years following the Triangle Shirtwaist Factory fire in 1911, New York Governor

Alfred E. Smith appointed her to the State Industrial Commission where she became a key contributor to the progressive initiatives of the Smith Administration, which then flowed into the initiatives of the administration of Governor Franklin Roosevelt and finally to the national level as a leading part of FDR's New Deal. Schiff shows that through pragmatic efforts, Perkins broke glass ceilings both for women and for progressive political principles.

Frances Perkins, like FDR and her closest Cabinet associate, Henry A. Wallace, was an Episcopalian. The relationship between her religious beliefs and her social reform policy commitments is explored in an essay by DONN MITCHELL, based upon his lecture to the Frances Perkins Day Observance at her home church, St. Andrew's, in Newcastle, Maine, on May 16, 2010: "Frances Perkins: Heart and Soul of the New Deal." Tracing her development from her student days at Mount Holyoke College, to her career as a social worker, to her practical leadership in New York State securing fire safety regulations following the Triangle fire, to her influential national role during the New Deal, Mitchell demonstrates how Frances Perkins's contributions to the nation were profoundly informed by her religious convictions. He analyzes the significance for her mature social and political views of her conversion as a young woman from the Congregationalism of her family to Episcopalianism.

Harry Hopkins was a fellow social worker with Miss Perkins in New York State during the administration of Governor Franklin Roosevelt. Upon Perkins's recommendation to President Roosevelt, Hopkins became part of the new Administration in Washington. The role he played in shaping the Social Security Act is outlined in this volume by his granddaughter, JUNE HOPKINS, author of *Harry Hopkins: Sudden Hero, Brash Reformer*. Harry Hopkins's ardent efforts to include unemployment insurance in the bill were successful, even if he was unsuccessful in pushing for a federally guaranteed jobs program "to cope with cyclical unemployment inherent in capitalism."

Both Perkins and FDR regarded this worthy goal as impracticable and unattainable in the then current political climate. What Hopkins did persuade FDR to establish, with Perkins's support, was the Works Progress Administration (WPA), which provided jobs for millions of unemployed Americans from 1935 to 1942.

KIRSTIN DOWNEY'S acclaimed biography, *The Woman Behind the New Deal: The Life and Legacy of Frances Perkins—Social Security, Unemployment Insurance, and the Minimum Wage*, has captured the remarkable life and contributions of Miss Perkins to the economic safety net we possess today. In her essay in this volume, Downey details the important role Secretary Perkins played in drafting and laying the groundwork for Social Security. Her skillful handling of FDR, her chairing of the Cabinet level Committee on Economic Security, and her effective advocacy in Congress to win passage of the bill was followed by her management of the implementation of Social Security. While her foes in Congress saw to it that the new system would not be housed in the Department of Labor, Secretary Perkins recommended to President Roosevelt the first three members of the Social Security Board who oversaw the new law. Although the independent Social Security Administration was created to manage the program, Secretary Perkins and the Department of Labor provided the initial nurturing, including financial support, for the new agency.

The first chair of the Social Security Board was JOHN GILBERT WINANT, the former Republican governor of New Hampshire and future U.S. Ambassador to Great Britain during World War II. Secretary Perkins recommended him to President Roosevelt to lead this crucial bipartisan effort to implement Social Security. We have included Winant's letter of resignation from the board, which he tendered so he could campaign for FDR in 1936 and support the new Social Security law against the strident attacks of his old gubernatorial colleague, the Republican presidential nominee, Alfred E. Landon.

LARRY DEWITT, historian of the Social Security Administration and author of *Social Security: A Documentary History*, describes the overwhelming challenge of setting up the organization to manage this new system that would eventually involve virtually all Americans. Focusing on Secretary Perkins's leadership role and those she engaged in the effort, including the crucial long-term contributions of her deputy, Arthur Altmeyer, DeWitt tells of the triumphs and tribulations of perhaps the most efficient federal bureaucracy ever created, from its first days to the present.

PAUL LASEWICZ demonstrates the significance for modern data management of the pioneering partnership between the federal government and IBM to handle the records required by the Social Security program. The press at the time described it as the largest bookkeeping job in the world. Initially utilizing the punch card technology developed by IBM in the 1920s, this government-business partnership prepared the way for the immense data management of the federal government during World War II and during the dramatic expansion of government and business in post-war America. As Lasewicz shows, Frances Perkins made the leap of faith for the government to use IBM to create and update on a lifetime basis individual wage records for the then estimated 26 million workers who would be part of the new Social Security system.

Next to Altmeyer, the person most associated with the long-term success of the Social Security program was Robert M. Ball, who spent 68 of the first 75 years of the program's life working for the Social Security Administration, including eleven years under three presidents as Commissioner. In his essay, JONATHAN BALL recalls the centrality of Social Security to the life of his father and to their entire family. Robert Ball continued to be the authority on and one of the most effective advocates for Social Security until his recent death at the age of 93.

In her highly regarded book, *The Battle for Social Security: From FDR's Vision to Bush's Gamble*, NANCY J. ALTMAN details the ongoing struggle over Social Security from before its passage to the present. In her essay, she delineates the impact of Social Security on Americans since 1935, in contrast to the fate of the elderly, dependent children, the unemployed, and the disabled in pre-New Deal America. She shows that Social Security is a life insurance policy, a disability insurance policy, and an old age annuity policy, with premiums paid for by American workers. Its opponents obscure its essence as insurance and want to regard it as a type of welfare entitlement, particularly for the poor. Altman presents the statistics on how crucial Social Security is for a vast proportion of Americans, not only the elderly and disabled, but also children, nine percent of whom are supported by Social Security— making it the largest and most generous federal children's program.

Building on his two major works, *Social Security in the 21st Century* and *The Generational Equity Debate*, ERIC R. KINGSON shows that the current Social Security debate is over the role of government and its relation to fundamental societal values. Kingson begins with FDR's framing of the challenge in adopting Social Security legislation: "We are compelled to employ the active interest of the Nation as a whole through government in order to encourage a greater security for each individual who composes it." The current opponents of Social Security, Kingson explains, have successfully framed the issue in terms of an entitlement problem involving affordability, solvency, and deficit reduction, as well as generational equity. Lost in this "frame" is the insurance Social Security provides *all* Americans facing three major life events: death of a parent or spouse, old age, and potentially disabling condition. Kingson suggests that the issue of Social Security's future needs to be framed in terms of protecting individuals, families, and the national community against the risks to which all of us are subject, in short, making explicit the fundamental value of our mutual responsibility to each other.

TERESA GHILARDUCCI, author of *When I'm Sixty-four: The Plot Against Pensions and the Plan to Save Them*, is a specialist on America's wounded retirement pension system. In her essay for this book, she analyzes the weakness of the 401(k)-defined contribution plans and the retrenchment or termination of defined benefit plans by employers, leaving employees with the likelihood of inadequate retirement income. Social Security remains the most stable part of the retirement system and deserves to be strengthened. Ghilarducci suggests a range of incentives that the government can offer to encourage retirement savings for people in all income categories (at present such incentives heavily favor those with the highest incomes). She also proposes a plan for Guaranteed Retirement Accounts that complements and supplements Social Security. In the same way that Social Security keeps consumption steady among retirees, Ghilarducci argues, the Guaranteed Retirement Accounts would keep saving steady during their working years.

JAMES K. GALBRAITH, prominent economist and critic of conventional thinking, rejects as nonsense the "framing" of a looming Social Security financial crisis because of future unfunded entitlements. Opponents of Social Security, comparing revenue and expenditure streams over very long periods of time (a method used for no other federal programs except Medicare), project huge, scary "deficit gaps" decades from now. In his essay explaining the basics of the federal budget, Galbraith shows that the federal government does not maintain a stock of cash on hand or a credit balance at the bank like private firms or private individuals. While Social Security obligations in an accounting sense represent long-term public sector liabilities, they are also long-term public assets. There are no legal limits on the nominal value of bonds issued by the U.S. Treasury. Suggesting that Social Security and Medicare should not be segregated from the federal budget, Galbraith charges that the projection of a Social Security "deficit" is done to mandate cuts in benefits by those opposed to Social Security. What matters for the long-range projections are demographics, technology, and economic growth, which he proceeds to analyze in terms of the likely strength of the American economy to meet its obligation to future retirees. He concludes that the federal government has the operational ability to make all payments as they come due "and could do so even if through some strange accounting mistake or trick one concluded that government liabilities exceed private assets."

The recently elected junior senator from Illinois addressed the Franklin and Eleanor Roosevelt Institute at the National Press Club in Washington during the year of the 70th anniversary of Social Security. James Roosevelt, Jr. introduced Senator BARACK OBAMA at the luncheon on April 26, 2005. FDR understood, Obama explained, that the freedom to pursue one's dreams is made possible by the nation's promise that if fate causes one to stumble or fall, "our larger American family will be there to lift us up; that if we are willing to share even a small amount of life's risks and rewards with each other, then we will all have the chance to achieve our God-given potential." He sketched the new risks facing families in the twenty-first century. In rejecting the privatization proposals being put before the nation by President Bush in 2005, Senator Obama observed that "just as the naysayers in Roosevelt's day told us that there was nothing we could do to help people help themselves, people in power today are telling us that instead of sharing the risks of this new economy, we should make them shoulder those risks on their own." He quoted a White House memo that somehow made its way out of the Bush White House: "For the first time in six decades," the memo observed, "the Social Security battle is one we can win. And in doing so, we can help transform the political and philosophical landscape of the country." In rejecting the privatization proposals, Senator Obama pledged himself to work to save Social Security. "In doing so, I think we will affirm our belief that we are all connected as one people, ready to share life's risks and rewards for the benefit of each and the good of all."

Finally, we have included the speech JAMES ROOSEVELT, JR., gave on the 75th anniversary of Social Security to the Retirement Research Consortium of the Social Security Administration at the National Press Club in Washington on August 6, 2010. Entitled "The Mythology of Fear," Roosevelt recalls his grandfather's memorable injunction in his Inaugural Address on March 4, 1933: "The only thing we have to fear is fear itself." He charges that the enemies of Social Security, whose arguments mirror those used against FDR by Alf Landon in the 1936 presidential campaign, have created a mythology of fear to create doubt in the American people that Social Security will still be there for them when they retire. In explaining the fundamental solvency of the Social Security system, with its $2.5 trillion trust fund (secured by U.S. Treasury bonds—and expected to grow to $4.3 trillion by 2023), Roosevelt believes that Social Security ought to be off the table of the President's National Commission on Fiscal Responsibility and Reform, better known as the Deficit Commission. While he lists some of the modest revisions being considered to secure the system beyond 2037 (there have been ten revisions since the system started in 1935), he insists on the inherent strengths of the system. He then warns that "If we let our fears rule our judgment we will undo the greatest government program in our history, one that has eliminated poverty for millions of Americans and supported millions of families in need."

A Promise to All Generations is going to press after the release of the report of President Obama's Deficit Commission. The essays in the book were written before the Commission's report was released. Those essays addressing the present public debate over Social Security reflect the anticipation of the report's conclusions rather than a precise response to its recommendations. Nonetheless, we hope this volume will contribute to a fuller appreciation of the choices facing the President and Congress—and the American people—as changes to the Social Security system are considered. By providing an historical perspective, rooted in an understanding of conditions faced by the elderly before and during the Great Depression and an appreciation for the spiritual, political, and human values embodied in the program, we hope the story of Social Security's development and its impact on American families over the past 75 years can inform the critical debate now underway. By highlighting the leadership role played by Secretary of Labor Frances

Perkins, we not only honor her profound contribution to the American people, but also suggest how one individual, who immersed herself in the conditions of the most vulnerable Americans in her time, educated herself on the practical policy choices that might strengthen such individuals and thereby increase the overall health of the American family. She remains a model for young people who are contemplating the most effective and rewarding ways they might choose to make significant contributions to their country's future.

I REMEMBER my grandmother—who probably didn't ever put much money in, got something like $70 a month—this was in the 1950s. I think it was probably the only income she had. She lived in a house with a wood cookstove and a cistern and outdoor plumbing and had a big garden. For one's birthday she might give you a dime or a quarter—a large sum for the time and for her income.

She spent some of that money on thread and handkerchiefs which she would crochet around. I still have and treasure them.

— LORLEE BARTOS —
DALLAS, TEXAS

America Before Social Security

ADAM COHEN

Adam Cohen is a Lecturer in Law at Yale Law School
and a former member of *The New York Times*
editorial board, as well as the author of *Nothing to Fear:
FDR's Inner Circle and the Hundred Days that Created
Modern America*. He is a special policy advisor to New
York Governor Andrew Cuomo. Cohen wrote the
introduction to the forthcoming new edition of *The
Roosevelt I Knew* by Frances Perkins.

*B*efore Social Security, America was a hard place in which to grow old. There were some private and state pension systems, but few people qualified for them, and the benefits were woefully inadequate. There were no 401(k)s, and most did not own their own homes. To survive, old people usually had no choice but to work—hoping they remained healthy enough to keep at it—until the day they died.[2]

The only old people worse off than the ones forced to work were those who needed to work but were not able to. When the Great Depression hit, many older people lost their jobs and could not find new ones. Often, they were despondent about it—and desperately worried about how they would survive.

In her memoir, *The Roosevelt I Knew*, Frances Perkins told the story of one such person, an "almost deaf, elderly lawyer" she knew, a Harvard graduate whose legal practice had failed because of the economic crisis. Thanks to the New Deal, he was lucky enough to get a public works job as an assistant caretaker at a small public park. Whenever Perkins saw him "he would always ask me to take a message to the President—a message of gratitude for a job which paid him fifteen dollars a week and kept him from starving to death. It was an honorable occupation that made him feel useful and not like a bum and a derelict, he would say with tears in his eyes."[3]

Many elderly people were not so fortunate. In the years before Social Security, people could almost count on being poor when they grew old. Studies by several states in the 1920s and 1930s found that nearly half of their residents who were older than 65 did not have even a subsistence income.[4]

Older Americans often had no alternative but to throw themselves on the mercy of their families and friends. State surveys in the early 1930s found that from 30 percent to 50 percent of people over 65 were supporting themselves through such acts of generosity. Impoverished older people who did not have family or friends who were willing or able to help had to turn to private charity. Many ended up in poorhouses, grim institutions that were home to desperate people who had no better alternative. Almost every state had one or more poorhouses in the 1930s, and the residents were overwhelmingly elderly. A study of Massachusetts's almshouses in 1910 found that 92 percent of the people who moved in were over the age of 60. It was an ignominious and threadbare end to a life of hard work and self-sufficiency.[5]

Older people were, of course, not the only victims of the Depression, and the Social Security Act was intended to provide assistance to other disadvantaged groups, notably those who had been thrown out of work. In the early 1930s, this was an enormous contingent: unemployment had reached as high as 25 percent, and jobs of any kind were scarce. The act set up a system of unemployment insurance, to help tide people over until the next job came along.

Progressives had been working for years to establish both old age and unemployment insurance programs. As early as the 1880s, Germany had an old age pension system to which workers contributed, and by the 1930s, many European countries had some kind of old age pension system. Americans were beginning to call for their country to adopt a similar program, led by European immigrants who were accustomed to this sort of a safety net in their native lands. Groups with names like the American Association for Old Age Security were forming and pressing elected officials to take action. There were also increasing calls for unemployment insurance, and some states were beginning to draft possible legislation.[6]

When Franklin Roosevelt was Governor of New York and Perkins was his Industrial Commissioner, they supported both old age and unemployment insurance. They had been unable to get these programs enacted at the state level, but when Roosevelt became President the time was suddenly right. Part of the reason was the power that came with controlling the White House, but the real driving force was the Great Depression.

With the economic collapse, destitution was everywhere. It was no longer hidden out of sight, on the other side of the tracks, or in the inner-city slums. Suddenly, desperate people could be seen everywhere, including in once solidly middle-class neighborhoods. In a 1962 speech, Perkins recalled that it was common to encounter families who had been evicted from their homes sitting on the sidewalk, surrounded by their meager possessions. "I saw goods stay on the sidewalk in front of the same house with the same weeping children on top of the blankets for 3 days before anybody came to relieve the situation!" she recalled.[7]

Faced with this sort of misery, a consensus was emerging that the government had to help those in need. This was a major change in national outlook. In the Herbert Hoover years, the nation had lived by a gospel of self-reliance, disdaining the idea that the government should help those who could not help themselves. People had a blind faith in business and the free market, and believed that those who were not succeeding had only themselves to blame. With a quarter of the workforce jobless, however, it was clear that many good people who wanted to work could not support themselves. The 1932 presidential election had largely been a referendum on whether the federal government should do more to help the Depression's victims, and Roosevelt's promise of a "New Deal" for America won in a landslide.

Perkins, who was in a better position than almost anyone else to know the dynamics, made it clear that it was the hard times of the 1930s that utterly changed the national landscape and made Social Security possible. "I've always said, and I still think we have to admit, that no matter how much fine reasoning there was about the old age insurance system and the unemployment insurance prospects—no matter how many people were studying it, or how many committees had ideas on the subject, or how many college professors had written theses on the subject—and there were an awful lot of them—the real roots of the Social Security Act were in the Great Depression of 1929," she insisted. "Nothing else would have bumped the American people into a Social Security system except something so shocking, so terrifying, as that depression."[8]

Roosevelt and Perkins had not been able to promote either old age insurance or unemployment insurance in 1933, the first year of the Administration. The legislative agenda had simply been too tightly packed—1933 was perhaps the busiest single year in the history of the American presidency. On the day Roosevelt was sworn in, all of the nation's banks had been closed, and the first order of business had been reviving the tottering banking system—which the Administration did with the Emergency Banking Act. The Administration had to try to revive the farm belt, which it did with the Agricultural Adjustment Act. It needed to stimulate industry, which it tried to do with the sweeping National Industrial Recovery Act. On the subject of aid to those in need, the Administration's first priority had been the Federal Emergency Relief Act, to get money immediately out to the states to the most destitute Americans, and large-scale public works, which Perkins and others had ensured were included in the National Industrial Recovery Act.

By 1934, however, there was finally a chance to act. There were a number of reasons the timing was right, beyond the important fact that the Administration was finally ready to turn to old age and unemployment insurance. With the Depression entering its fourth year, the nation was ready for bold action—and more sweeping social welfare programs. The first year of the New Deal had prompted all sorts of criticism on the right—charges of Socialism and Bolshevism. One congressional wit declared that the Agricultural Adjustment Act was so difficult to understand because it had been translated from the original Russian. Roosevelt's own budget director had morosely warned that the President's policies would lead to the end of Western Civilization. Despite the often vitriolic criticism, the majority of Americans were telling their elected officials that they wanted the New Deal to go further.

There were a few especially outspoken public figures clamoring for Roosevelt to do more—people the historian Alan Brinkley has called the "voices of protest." Huey Long, the Louisiana populist, was savagely attacking Roosevelt for doing too little for the workingman, and threatening to run for President himself in 1936. Father Charles Coughlin, the hate-spewing radio preacher, was delivering spellbinding speeches to an audience of millions denouncing Roosevelt for being too close to Wall Street.

Some of the most influential of these populist critics aimed squarely at the Administration's failure to take care of the elderly. When Upton Sinclair ran for governor of California in 1934, he proposed $50-a-month pensions for everyone who had lived in the state for at least three years. Frances Townsend, a 66-year-old California doctor, had begun a national campaign for old age pensions. His "Townsend Clubs" were popping up all over the country and were having a powerful impact. By January of 1934, there were 5,000 of them, promoting Dr. Townsend's program of a $200-a-month pension for everyone over the age of 60. In time, Townsend would produce 20 million petition signatures demanding that the federal government establish old age pensions.[9]

The congressional landscape was also more auspicious than ever. Incumbent parties usually lose seats, but in the 1934 midterm elections, the Democrats had actually increased their already sizeable majorities in both houses. Faced with the question of whether the federal government should do more or less, the voters emphatically chose more. Members of Congress wanted new programs that they could bring back to their constituents to show that the government was doing everything it could to combat the hard times.

One of the most auspicious things of all about the landscape, of course, was that Perkins was there in the Cabinet to fight for Social Security. There were other members of Roosevelt's inner circle pushing for old age pensions, including Harry Hopkins, who was heading up the federal relief program and playing a large role in directing public works. There were also skeptics, notably Henry Morgenthau, the fiscally conservative Treasury Secretary, who was channeling the business community—which was digging in its heels. The National Association of Manufacturers was calling the Social Security bill "the ultimate socialistic control of life and industry" and urged its allies in Congress to block it.

There was no champion like Perkins—the woman Roosevelt would appoint to chair the committee that got the ball rolling on Social Security. No one in the Roosevelt Administration was more knowledgeable about the intricacies of old age pensions, and no one more passionately committed to helping those in need. There was also no one in the Cabinet who went back further with Roosevelt, or had talked with him longer about the importance of social insurance.

Perkins also had another key strength: a supreme unwillingness to be bowled over by critics. At a church in New York City in early 1935, when Perkins was barnstorming for the proposed Social Security Act, a young woman complained during the question and answer period that Karl Marx proposed the same kind of unemployment insurance and old age pensions on page 30 of the Communist Manifesto. "How can you support such a program when you know that it is the same as Marx's?" the woman asked.

"I am supporting it," Perkins responded, "because I'd rather see it as a reality than on page 30."

NEXT TO MY bed I have an old prayer book from the early twentieth century. The black and worn book was my great grandfather's. I never knew him; he passed in the midst of the Great Depression of 1933. Grandpa Edward was of Irish ancestry, muscular, hard working, and fun loving.

As I leaf through the pages of prayers, poems, and photos, I often wonder what thoughts and ideas crossed his mind in those turbulent years.

Great-grandmother Katie was also of Irish ancestry, small, educated, determined, and probably ahead of the times on women's rights.

Ed and Katie owned a small farm and dairy business west of Lancaster, Wisconsin. In addition they also housed and cared for one daughter and three younger grandchildren. These were tough times and everyone relied on each other for care and support.

Early in the 1930s, money was becoming very scarce. There was never enough to live on, after paying the bills and credit obligations. By 1933, the farm and business fell to the creditors. Probably due to his age and all of the financial factors of stress and strain posed by the economic upheaval, Edward died.

Katie and the kids started looking at options to survive as an intact family. Ed had a small Catholic Knights of Columbus

Insurance policy. Also Katie had a sister in town, Jody, with a house that they were able to take shelter in. Then in 1935, thanks to the Roosevelt Administration and Frances Perkins, the Social Security System was established. At 68, Katie was able to apply and receive Social Security as one of the first recipients.

As the Depression continued, the occupants supplemented their incomes with room rentals and food preparation for the temporary WPA and CCC workers that had come to the Lancaster area for employment.

As time passed Katie was able to stabilize the financial situation for the family. Sometime later in the 1930s or 1940s, the family sold the present house and moved to a larger house, which allowed for home dining and a catering business.

If it had not been for the development of Social Security it is hard to imagine what would have happened to Ed and Katie's extended family. I believe when severe disasters, wars, or a financial catastrophe develop, only a government has the power, know-how, or financial soundness to keep a country and its people afloat.

— Tom Bartling —
Janesville, Wisconsin

An Advocate Comes of Age

KARENNA GORE SCHIFF

During the writing of her book, *Lighting the Way: Nine Women Who Changed Modern America*, Karenna Gore Schiff became fascinated with the story of Frances Perkins. She has continued that interest by co-creating a short documentary about Perkins. The eldest daughter of Vice President Al Gore, Schiff previously worked as the director of Community Affairs for the Association to Benefit Children (ABC). Before that, she was an attorney at Simpson Thacher and Bartlett. Her other work experience includes freelance writing and positions on the editorial staffs of *Slate* magazine in Redmond, Washington, and *El Pais* newspaper in Madrid, Spain.

*F*rances Perkins's journey from the shy daughter of conservative New Englanders to the powerful policy maker who fundamentally changed the relationship between the American government and its workforce is a fascinating example of how an individual's character can be so matched to a moment in history that they have the chance to write a piece of it themselves. Her roots—ancestors who were heroes of the American Revolution, relatives who espoused "Yankee" values—and her rigorous, advanced education combined with an innate sense of empathy to steer her toward public service. She came of age just as a network of women social workers were effectively pressing a progressive political agenda that amounted to a humanist response to the Industrial Revolution. As she was propelled to the top tier of political power, Frances Perkins not only broke glass ceilings for women, she broke them for principles. Concepts that grew out of contemporary social work, such as the necessity of care for the elderly and relief for the unemployed, went from being feminine adjuncts to government to essential components of public policy.

As a child, Perkins was steeped in her family's American heritage— her paternal grandmother, Cynthia Otis, to whom she was particularly close, was descended from James Otis, the revolutionary war hero known for his arguments against "taxation without representation."

His sister, Mercy Otis Warren, was a savvy, scholarly confidante of the founding fathers and a writer who authored political plays and the first history of the Revolutionary War. Young Fannie (her given name) equated resistance to exploitation with patriotism, and soon came to view unfettered commercialism as antithetical to the founding principles of the United States. Even her trademark tricorn hat—which her mother had picked out for her when she was a child to flatter her wide face—seemed to mark her as a keeper of the flame.

It was at Mount Holyoke College at the turn of the century that Fannie Perkins first came face to face with industrial workers. Perkins took particular interest in studies that resonated with her nascent social conscience, which had been fueled by reading Jacob Riis's historic *How the Other Half Lives*, as a teenager. (Riis used the new technology of flash photography to document urban tenement life and wrote about horrid realities, such as a young boy who starved to death because his father couldn't work due to lead poisoning.) When her history professor, Annah May Soule, took students to record their observations of working conditions in nearby factories, it "opened the door to the idea that the lack of comfort and security in some people was not solely due to the fact that they drank, which had been the prevailing view in my parental society."

This firsthand exposure to industrial life was soon followed by an introduction to political organization by women—and to the figure who might have had the biggest impact on Perkins's career, Florence Kelley. The National Consumer's League sought to abolish sweatshops and child labor by convincing the public not to patronize businesses profiting from them. Because women made most of the buying decisions, its mission also sought to give them a political voice. The girls at Mount Holyoke organized their own chapter of the NCL and on February 20, 1902, its president, Florence Kelley, came to speak to them.

In his biography of Perkins, *Madam Secretary Frances Perkins,* George Martin writes that Kelley's "dynamic personality, her practical experience, her demand for dramatic improvement, and the 'sense of crusade' surrounding her all appealed to Fannie." The daughter of a famous progressive congressman and niece of abolitionist Sarah Pugh, Kelley was a fiery speaker with reams of experience to back up her allegations and a clear prescription for the problem. Perkins later wrote that she "took a whole group of young people formless in their aspirations, and molded their aspirations for social justice into some definite purpose, into a program that had meaning and that had experience and that had practicality at the back of it."

Seeking that meaning, experience, and practicality, Perkins delved into the world of settlement houses, the homes and community centers created by women like Lillian Wald of New York and Jane Addams of Chicago, to assist and advocate for the immigrant poor. She had to teach at private girls' schools to make a living but focused on her volunteer work in these institutions, and clearly viewed it as the honorable extension of her education. She wrote to the Mount Holyoke alumnae update that she "ran the most interesting Girl's Club" at one settlement house in Worcester, Massachusetts. "Girls from 14 to 16 and most of them working in factories and stores already. We meet twice a week now and on one night we have gymnasium work and gym games—they are all hollow-chested and never get any exercise after being cramped up all day."

In one particularly affecting episode, one of these girls, Mary Hogan, had her hand cut off by a candy-dipping machine in the factory where she worked. The management simply bandaged her up and sent her home, without any semblance of treatment or support. Perkins took up her cause, but only ended up securing one hundred dollars in compensation.

Perkins continued her two-pronged approach when she moved to Chicago, teaching physics and biology at Ferry Hall in Lake Forest, Illinois, and working as much as she could at the flagship of settlement houses, Jane Addam's Hull House. It was during these years that her sense of mission came into sharper focus; she met people who seemed to envision a deeper solution to the circumstances of people like Mary Hogan and wanted to join them. "I had to do something about unnecessary hazards to life, unnecessary poverty," she explained, "This feeling . . . sprang out of a period of great philosophical confusion which overtakes all young people."

Addams was from a large well-off Midwestern family: her father was a Civil War veteran, politician, and friend of Abraham Lincoln (who addressed him in letters as "My Dear Double D'ed Addams)." Brought up with an emphasis on civic affairs, she found the inspiration for her work on a trip to London where she saw students from Oxford and Cambridge working with the poor at Toynbee Hall in the East End. When she returned to the United States in 1889, she and her friend Agnes Starr leased Hull House in Chicago's Nineteenth District where people lived with horrid sanitation, overcrowding, high unemployment, crime, and exploitation.

Jane Addams's charisma and intellect drew people to Hull House and sustained a warm but intentional culture. Florence Kelley began her career there. Dr. Alice Hamilton, who ran the "well-baby" clinic, described Addams's '"mixture of sweetness and aloofness, of sympathetic understanding and impersonality, and the total absence of that would-be-charm and false intimacy which school and college had made me dislike heartily in older women." And above all, Addams believed that social theory meant nothing if it did not produce positive results. "Truth must be put to the ultimate test: the test of the conduct it dictates and inspires."

Addams assigned Perkins to secure wages that were being unjustly withheld from the poor immigrants, an experience that opened her eyes to how powerless these people were as individuals against industrial power. She, who had been brought up to believe that "unions were an evil to be avoided," came to a firm conviction that "unions were the only powerful force to stand up for these individuals and make sure they were paid the wages they had earned." Moreover, Perkins's patriotism was sparked by a sense that the Hull House approach was manifestly democratic. "Miss Addams taught us to take all the elements of the community into conference for the solution to any human problem— the grasping politician, the corner saloon-keeper, the policeman on the beat, the president of the University, the head of the railroad, the labor leader, all cooperating through the latent desire for association which is the American genius."

While in Chicago, Perkins also made two significant changes to her identity. She changed her name from Fannie to Frances and left the Congregational for the Episcopal Church. There was a more formal nature to both of these changes that seems to reflect how much more seriously she was taking herself as a self-made figure who could move easily in different strata of society. And as Kirstin Downey has pointed out in her biography, *The Woman Behind the New Deal*, the name Frances was gender neutral, which may have deflected some obstacles, at least on paper, and the Episcopalian faith gave her access to a network of more socially prominent friends who would prove valuable allies in her work. In any event, it was a striking declaration of independence and purpose.

In 1907, Perkins decided to leave teaching behind for professional social work and more education, and began to push the boundaries of what she could achieve in that field. She took a job as the executive secretary of the Philadelphia Research and Protective Association, which helped girls who had been lured into brothels. Working with the police and courts—something she learned from settlement house life—she successfully put some sex traffickers out of business, and saved the lives of countless women who some in polite society would have considered beyond reach.

After studying sociology and economics at the University of Pennsylvania, she was awarded a fellowship to the New York School of Philanthropy at Columbia University "in the very heart of both the theoretical and practical efforts to socialize the life of the modern city." She moved into a settlement house in Hell's Kitchen in order to complete her research project on malnutrition among urban children and began working with Tammany Hall politicians such as Thomas "The" McManus, known as "the devil's deputy."

Frances was building on her experience working within the system, growing increasingly comfortable with elected officials, no matter how corrupt or imperfect. The year she was awarded a Columbia masters degree in political science, her thesis concluded: "Temporary relief is necessary and its method may well deserve discussion, but it is after all only an expedient to head off malnutrition until society adjusts itself and provides adequate incomes and adequate education to all its workers."

In 1910, she became the executive chairman of the New York Consumer's League, which had been organized by Lillian Wald, and operated under the national NCL, still chaired by Florence Kelley. Frances described Kelley as "a firebrand and a driver . . . but there was something sweeping and cleansing in her anger. She was never little, never mean. 'Frances,' she would say, 'you have got to do it.' Then she would give me that steely look." A decade had passed since Frances Perkins was mesmerized by Florence Kelley's speaking to her class at Mount Holyoke; now she was her colleague. Soon, their work would land Frances on her first political stage.

It was in her capacity as chairman of the New York Consumer's League that Perkins began an investigation of the safety of factories (the census reported about 26,000 of them in New York at the time), specifically with regard to fire. Fire codes were minimal, resulting in many tragic events, including a factory fire on November 26, 1910, that killed 25 people and injured 40. Perkins was still operating in the wake of that disaster, urging companies to adopt their own stricter safeguards, when an unprecedented tragedy struck.

On Saturday, March 25, 1911, on the northwest corner of Washington

Place and Greene Street, a fire broke out in the Triangle Shirtwaist Factory. The one fire escape soon collapsed and hundreds of workers were desperately trying to escape. Frances Perkins was having tea with a friend in nearby Washington Square and walked toward the commotion. "Without saying much of anything," she recalled, "we all went down the steps and just went toward the fire. It was about that time that they began to jump. It was the most horrible sight." One hundred forty-six workers died that day, most of them young immigrant women.

In the days after the fire, it was revealed that there had been no fire drills, the doors were regularly locked, there were oily sewing machines crammed together, and piles of flammable scraps on the ground. The nature of the grief was shaped by the fact that reformers had been pressing for safeguards to prevent exactly what happened. In what Perkins later described as the most moving speech she ever heard, Rose Schneiderman of the Shirtwaist Makers union said, "We have tried you good people of the public and found you wanting . . . This is not the first time girls have been burned alive in this city . . . The life of men and women is so cheap and property is so sacred . . . You have a couple of dollars for the sorrowing mothers and brothers and sisters by way of a charity gift. But every time the workers come out in the only way they know how to protest against conditions which are unbearable, the strong hand of the law is allowed to press down heavily upon us."

Indeed, the courts found that the owner of the building had complied with the law and was innocent. The owners of the company were acquitted of all charges and collected $65,000 from their insurance company, about $445 for each dead employee.

For Frances Perkins, this was a classic example of how the United States was in danger of becoming the sort of oppressive regime that her ancestors had fought against. The fact that the oppression was commercial brings to mind Napoleon's famous scoff that Britain was an unworthy "nation of shopkeepers"; Perkins's family's "Yankee values" included the concept that the human dignity of working-class Americans trumped the financial bottom line of industrial titans. She was poised to build on the response to the Industrial Revolution that was largely pioneered by women social activists like Schneiderman. The fiery labor leader Mother Jones wrote an open letter to Theodore Roosevelt in 1903, "We ask you, Mr. President, if our commercial greatness has not cost us too much by being built on the quivering hearts of helpless children." Jones's crusade against child labor was not ultimately successful until Perkins became Secretary of Labor, a road paved by her deft reaction to the Triangle fire.

The public outcry resulted in the formation of the New York State Factory Investigating Commission which was chaired by state Senator Robert Wagner, with Assemblyman Al Smith as the vice chair. Perkins was called to testify. After impressing everyone with her knowledge and analysis, she was appointed director of investigations. Kirstin Downey explains that former President Teddy Roosevelt, who had grown considerably more progressive in his political views, played a role in her appointment; he had undoubtedly heard of her through Florence Kelley and Jane Addams and recommended her to the man in charge of forming the commission. Under Perkins's leadership the commission not only examined fire safety, it reported on, in her words, "all kinds of human conditions that were unfavorable to employees, including long hours, including low wages, including the labor of children, including the overwork of women, including homework put out by the factories to be taken home by women."

The women social reformers before her, Mother Jones, Jane Addams, Florence Kelley, Rose Schneiderman, Lillian Wald, Alice Hamilton, to name a few, had taken it upon themselves to do this kind of work outside of government. Alice Hamilton, a physician who pioneered the field of "industrial medicine," studying the effect of chemicals and machinery on factory workers and recommending safeguards, said she felt a responsibility to go into that field because so many male doctors rejected it as "tainted with Socialism or feminine sentimentality for the poor."

Because Perkins had learned to apply her knowledge and experience to problems while working within the system, she was able to characterize work that formally had this "taint" as mainstream politics. "Factory inspection is of vast importance," she noted, "not only to the people who work in the factories, but to the entire community, and such work well done may be looked upon as a service to one's country."

Her impact was felt immediately, especially through the eyes of New York's elevated officials. She recalled:

> We used to make it our business to take Al Smith, the East Side boy who later became New York's governor and a presidential candidate, to see the women, thousands of them, coming off the ten-hour night shift on the rope walks in Auburn. We made sure that Robert Wagner personally crawled through the tiny hole in the wall that gave egress to a steep iron ladder covered with ice and ending twelve feet from the ground, which was euphemistically labeled 'Fire Escape' in many factories. We saw to it that the austere legislative members of the commission got up with us at dawn and drove with us for an unannounced visit to a Cattauraugus County cannery and that they saw with their own eyes the little children, not adolescents, but five-, six-, and seven-year-olds, snipping beans and shelling peas. We made sure that they saw the machinery that would scalp a girl or cut off a man's arm.

Perkins's commission issued its final report in 1915, recommending legislative changes to remedy these conditions. Al Smith called his tenure on the commission "the greatest education he'd ever had." Its findings and recommendations would help shape his initiatives when he became governor a few years later.

During this time, Perkins was also lobbying for the 54 Hour bill, which would change New York State law to limit the working hours of women and boys under 18 to 54 hours per week. Again, she relished working within the system. She worked with Tammany's "Big Tim" Sullivan who represented the lower east side. "He was real," she said, "you didn't have to show him statistics on the incidence of fatigue poisoning to make him understand that a girl's back aches if she works too much."

Perkins agreed to several changes in order to get the votes needed for the bill, including an exemption for the canning industry. The fact that Florence Kelley's potential reaction was first and foremost in Perkins's mind underscores the deep influence Kelley had on her. "At that moment, I became an adult. I pictured Mrs. Kelley's face when I brought the work in. I thought of all she would say. I was terrified but I thought, yes, let us take what we can get." On March 27, 1912, the bill passed (eleven years after Mother Jones's children's march). To Perkins surprise, Kelley threw her arms around her and said "Frances, Frances, we have won; you have done it!" without a word of rebuke. Frances had already absorbed pragmatism as a cardinal virtue that included making difficult compromises; in a friend's words, she became a "half-loaf girl; take what you can get now and try for more later."

By this point, Frances had developed good rapport with male politicians, due in part to her cultivation of a matronly type of femininity that would appeal to their conscience. "The way men take women in political life is to associate them with motherhood," she explained. "They know and respect their mothers—ninety-nine percent of them do. It's a primary and primitive attitude. I said to myself, 'That's the way to get things done. So behave, so dress, and so comport yourself that you remind them of their mothers.'" This was reminiscent of Mother Jones's approach—she always dressed in long conservative dresses, exaggerated her age, and called the workers she addressed her "boys," not to mention completely embracing "Mother" in place of her given name, Mary.

Perkins employed this traditional affect while challenging gender norms. In 1913, she married Paul Wilson, an economist and assistant secretary to reform Mayor John Purroy Mitchel who *The New Yorker* magazine described as "one of the most civilized and intelligent men on Manhattan island." Wilson later became debilitated by mental illness. Perkins kept her maiden name. "My whole generation," she said, understating her exceptionalism, "was, I suppose, the first generation that openly and actively asserted—at least some of us did—the separateness of women and their personal independence in the family relationship." What Perkins did within her own family was soon writ large on political society.

After her first-born child died following birth, Perkins became executive secretary of the Maternity Center Association, which sought to improve infant and maternal health care. She then had a daughter, Susanna. Perkins soon took the final step wedding social work to politics by joining Al Smith's 1918 campaign for governor. She had already established a good working relationship with Smith from their joint service on the Factory Investigating Commission and their collaboration to push for the 54 Hour bill. Smith had taken an interest in her career, advising her on procedural strategy, urging her to speak on behalf of women's suffrage, and suggesting that she become a Democrat (a switch from her Independent status, which she maintained even before women had the vote). "Good people need to be in the party, not outside looking in," she remembered him saying, "then they have some influence. Then the party takes up a good and wise program."

When Smith won, Perkins was definitely on the inside and her contemporaries understood the significance. The newly elected governor appointed Perkins to the State Industrial Commission, a position unprecedented for a woman. Upon hearing the news, Florence Kelley burst into tears, exclaiming, "Glory be to God, you don't mean it. I never thought I would live to see the day when someone we had trained, and whom we knew knew about industrial conditions, cared about women, cared to have things right, would be an administrative officer." Only a woman with as impeccable a resume as Perkins could have broken such ground. When people objected, Smith replied, "I appointed Miss Perkins because of her ability and her knowledge of the department of labor and statutes affecting labor. She was very active in the legislative investigation that led to the labor code."

Frances distinguished herself in the position, skillfully defusing a copper worker's strike in 1919, and working well with people across the state. When Smith lost in 1920, Perkins took a job as executive secretary of the Council on Immigrant Education, but it was clear she would be back in the political arena soon. And indeed, when Smith won back the governorship in 1922, she resumed her post. When he unsuccessfully ran for the Democratic nomination for president in 1924, she chaired the platform committee of the Women's Democratic Union.

As Al Smith's progressive administration gained traction, Perkins pushed forward policies that foreshadowed the New Deal. When she became head of the Industrial Commission, she described it as "the perfect job" because she could make "constant progress toward practical achievement of social justice." For her that meant adopting codes that made people responsible for hazards in the workplace. For example, she championed a law that made the manufacturers of chemicals responsible for toxic side effects, explaining that they would change their ways when they found out that "it costs money to poison people."

A British reporter observed in the *Manchester Guardian*, "I have met a considerable number and wide range of interesting women in the United States but none who has impressed me more than this squarely built woman . . . Under her guidance a comprehensive and enlightened factory code is being worked out and applied, which is transforming factory and workshop conditions as they affect the safety, health, and comfort of the worker; and worked out largely in friendly cooperation with the use of the most up-to-date scientific counsel and advice from engineering and other experts."

It was during the 1928 Smith presidential campaign that Franklin

Roosevelt arrived as a major national figure, coming forcefully into the spotlight seven years after being stricken with polio. When Smith lost the presidential election to Herbert Hoover, Roosevelt took his place as governor. Eleanor wrote her husband: "I hope you will consider making Frances Perkins labor commissioner. She would do so well and you could fill her place as chair of the Industrial Commission with one of the men."

When FDR did so, he began a professional partnership that changed history. Perkins brought her experience and convictions to his gubernatorial administration and beyond. Frances Perkins would later recall FDR saying, "Practically all the things we've done in the federal government are like things Al Smith did as Governor of New York."

On January 22, 1930, in the middle of the despair that followed the stock market crash that fall, President Hoover announced that the economy was improving. Perkins gathered her own group of experts to look at the unemployment figures in New York and project a national analysis, which definitively showed that things were getting worse. She called a widely publicized press conference of her own, a bold move that FDR applauded: "Bully for you . . . I probably would not have told you to do it, and I think it is much more wholesome to have it out in the open." Perkins became a nationally known expert on unemployment; she quickly advised FDR to appoint a committee to study it.

On October 2, 1930, Eleanor Roosevelt wrote her husband: "Miss Perkins came to see me today and she has a secret offer which will be made if you agree. The commission she got together to look into the public employment department will recommend if you are agreeable that a commission similar to the old age pension one be appointed. . . . It looks good to me for it would take into account middle aged and physically handicapped, etc. and let you get the jump on Hoover, but they won't move until you tell me what you think."

Perkins's Industrial Commission's recommendations foreshadowed much of the New Deal: reducing working hours so that more workers could be hired, developing government sponsored work projects. Its report concluded: "the public conscience is not comfortable when good men anxious to work are unable to find employment to support themselves and their families." In January of 1931, FDR called a multistate conference on unemployment, which helped provide the major theme of his historic 1932 campaign for President. Perkins provided constant information and policy suggestions for the campaign and was his clear choice to lead one of the most critical parts of his Administration as Secretary of Labor, a position she held for his entire tenure as President.

Frances Perkins was remarkably receptive to a unique moment in history, gathering knowledge about socioeconomic conditions and how to improve them for the most vulnerable and then challenging the government to take on that role, just as the human toll of an unregulated Industrial Revolution came into the spotlight. She saw social work as a pure form of public service and promoted it as such. What astonished people like Florence Kelley about Perkins's rise to the top was that she was making traditionally feminine concerns part of the mainstream political agenda. It was no longer just Mount Holyoke students examining the most dismal industrial scenes; now public officials and journalists paid increasing attention to these problems.

Perkins said that one of the women reformers she most admired, Jane Addams, taught her that "the latent desire for association" between people from all walks of life was part of "the American genius." It was certainly part of Frances's genius. She spent her days of public service moving between presidents and assembly line workers, wealthy philanthropists and the lowest paid prostitutes. She sought to redeem the dignity and opportunity of those left indigent by exploitation, and in doing so brought the nation closer to the democratic ideal that her revolutionary ancestors had imagined.

ALTHOUGH MONEY can never replace the love and guidance of a parent, the reality of life is such that money is needed in order to survive. In November of 2003, I lost my 28-year-old son in an accident just eight days after he became a father for the first time. Eight days was all he had with his son; eight days to love his infant child. That little boy is now six years old, lives with his Mom in southern Maine, and although he is growing up without his Daddy, his small family is secure in the fact that each month a check will arrive from the Social Security Administration to help defray living expenses.

That small boy will never know his Dad or share the special memories that define the man he will become. He will never share with his Dad the thrill of walking through the woods on junior hunting day in search of the great white-tailed deer; the thrill of casting his line into the waters to catch the ever elusive trout; or learning how to drive on the back roads of Maine. He will learn truth, honesty, and the American spirit from someone else. I am saddened that my son is no longer with us; I am saddened that my grandson has to grow up without his Daddy; but I am grateful that a program which began 75 years ago still exists today to help struggling families deal financially with the loss of a loved one.

Could one have imagined that a program begun in the 1930s during the Roosevelt Administration would still be providing financial support three-quarters of a century later to millions of Americans across this country? Matthew will only know his Daddy through the memories of others, but he will always know that Social Security will be there for him until he becomes a young man, all because socially conscious people like Frances Perkins and Franklin Roosevelt had a vision for the care of America's elderly and its needy children. What a legacy!

—ANGELA N. STOCKWELL
ATHENS, MAINE

said th...
Wall Street ...
to be named.

Nasdaq officials said the halt was prompted by a problem with the data system that disseminates prices, and that its cause had been addressed.

Two days earlier, Goldman Sachs accidentally sent out a barrage of errant trades that disrupted the exchanges where options are bought and sold. The two episodes have amplified questions about the reliability and integrity of financial markets that companies depend on to raise money and Americans trust with their retirement savings

More than a year ago, the eagerly awaited market debut of

"flash crash"
stocks plunged to
the Dow Jones ind
age plummeted mo
points in a matter o.

While regulator
ket participants hav
eral steps to streng
systems, the prob
week suggest that t
the markets have n
paired, and may act
ting worse.

"You have a very
berg system", said C
cofounder of the bro
Abel/Noser. "We'v
patches on it withou
the basic problems."

The persistence o

most rece... ...eteller Institute
of Government, which tracks state and local finances.

Who should own municipal bonds?

Income payments made by municipal bonds
are free from taxes, so taxpayers in the highest
brackets get the biggest after-tax boost.

BMO's McAllister says municipal bonds make
sense for investors in the 28 percent income-tax
bracket and above. For a single filer, that means
anyone with taxable income of more than
$87,850. For a married couple filing jointly, that
means making more than $146,400.

Who shouldn't own municipal bonds?

Investors looking to put money to work in
their 401(k) or other tax-deferred account. That
would be a missed opportunity to benefit from
putting taxable investments like stocks or corporate bonds in those accounts.

Frances Perkins and the Spiritual Foundation of the New Deal

DONN MITCHELL

Donn Mitchell teaches religion and ethics at Berkeley College in New York and edits The Anglican Examiner (www.AnglicanExaminer.com), a religion and public affairs website. He has written widely on the spiritual life of Frances Perkins and the religious dimension of the New Deal. His father and three of his grandparents lived out their retirement years with Social Security as their sole source of income, and his 86-year-old mother continues to do the same. Most Social Security recipients are senior citizens who have paid into the system for decades. The average recipient works 37 years before collecting his or her first check.

*U*nder Franklin Delano Roosevelt, the nation experienced the longest and arguably the most popular presidential Administration in U.S. history. Elected to office four times, the consensus Roosevelt forged, known as the New Deal, dominated U.S. politics from 1932 to 1980, producing the closest thing to social democracy the United States has ever seen. Frances Perkins, the heart and soul of New Deal social policy, made history as the first woman to be appointed to a Presidential Cabinet. As the principal architect of the Social Security system, she lifted millions of people out of poverty, and forty-five years after her death she continues to help in ways that are less apparent.

Consider the tragedy of September 11, 2001, for example. Consider how it dramatically illustrated first the worst and then the best of human possibilities. An outpouring of sacrificial love of stranger for stranger followed the horror of innocent people being used as weapons to kill other innocent people. This love was present in the individuals who risked or lost their lives to rescue others. It was present in those who set aside their life's priorities to work at Ground Zero in the aftermath and in still others who volunteered at St. Paul's Chapel to provide aid and comfort to the rescue workers.

For countless others, love expressed itself in the donation of more than $500 million to the survivors. For these donors, money became a means of expressing their innermost feelings—an outward and visible sign of love for people they had never known. Sadly, though, these donations quickly became mired in controversy, amid accusations that the groups receiving them were distributing too little to the victims and taking too long to do it.

But there is one group who began to receive cash payments almost immediately. Some 11,000 children who lost a parent in the September 11 attacks began receiving Social Security payments as soon as their parents' deaths were confirmed. The payments will continue until the youngest of these children turns eighteen. Although it is never described as such, this too is the result of an act of love from many years ago.

Frances Perkins, rightly called the mother of the U.S. Social Security system, believed insurance was the most moral concept humankind had ever developed because it harnessed the generous impulse of neighbor to help neighbor with human technical skill in the form of actuarial science. By applying human intelligence to the best aspect of the human spirit, neighbor could help neighbor even before tragedy struck.

Although it never paraded under the banner of a particular religious group, the cause of social insurance was a religious quest for Perkins, and she made its inclusion in the New Deal agenda a condition of her participation as Secretary of Labor. Like many American Episcopalians of her day, Perkins was steeped in the socialist thought of British Anglo-Catholicism. This viewpoint combined Anglicanism's traditionally affirmative view of the state as the instrument through which the community expresses its shared values with an emphasis on the compassionate elements of Catholic tradition.

For Perkins, social insurance, i.e., state-sponsored insurance for virtually all citizens, was both a secularization and a socialization of what Catholic tradition knows as the seven Corporal Works of Mercy: 1) to feed the hungry; 2) to give drink to the thirsty; 3) to clothe the naked; 4) to harbor the harborless; 5) to visit the sick; 6) to ransom the captive; and 7) to bury the dead.

In a premodern economy, such as Medieval Europe, these merciful deeds would have been executed in kind, that is, a hungry person would be given food. But in the money economy that evolved in the early modern period, mercy itself was "monetarized." Instead of giving food from agricultural surplus, a work of mercy might consist of putting money into the hands of those who would otherwise lack the means to acquire food. The same was true for shelter and the other necessities of life.

The original vision of Social Security, which included health insurance, addressed most of these works of mercy. As it was finally enacted, the law extended unemployment and workers compensation insurance to most workers, retirement pensions to virtually all elderly citizens, death benefits to cover burial expenses, aid to families with dependent children, and stipends for children who lost a wage-earning parent. By guaranteeing income to persons who were no longer able to work or otherwise pay their way, the law combined the Catholic ideals of mercy with the long-standing Protestant emphasis on personal responsibility. To *give* was an act of mercy. To give *money* was to help people help themselves.

This concept also resonated deeply with Jewish ethical traditions. The idea that the employer should pay half the worker's wages during times of involuntary unemployment is clearly articulated in the Talmud, as is the assertion that the employer should compensate workers or their descendants for workplace injuries.

Of all the things Perkins and her colleagues wanted it to be, there is one thing Social Security was never intended to be. It was never intended to be an investment program. It was never intended to be a state-sponsored plan for accumulating personal wealth. The current debate, framed as a math problem, obscures the historical reality that the very juxtaposition of the terms "social" and "security" was a statement about the nature of community.

In February of 1948, as New York shoveled its way out of a record-breaking blizzard, Frances Perkins delivered a series of lectures at

St. Thomas, Fifth Avenue. At the end of one of the lectures, a man in the audience asked, "Don't you think it's wrong for people to get things they don't pay for?"

"Why no," Perkins responded. "I find I get so much more than I pay for. Don't you?"

In a succinct way, she was revealing both her own theological perspective as well as the moral values that informed the New Deal. She knew she had not paid for the earth she walked on or the parents who had raised her. She had not "earned" the breath in her lungs. All life was an unearned gift from God, as she saw it.

What we "got," in her view, was a function of grace, not merit or its inverse correlate, sin. A godly society, in her view, would be a *gracious* society. Just as God had endowed us with the basics and then allowed us freedom to develop our capacities to create and contribute, so the community should graciously guarantee basic provision for its individual members while allowing them maximum freedom to make their way in the world.

In promoting the Social Security Act when it was before Congress in 1935, Perkins described it as something of a "departure" for Americans. It was a departure in at least two ways. Just as the Puritans had understood the universal church *congregationally* rather than globally, Americans had tended to understand community locally. Indeed, social welfare needs had been a county responsibility ever since the young republic had dismantled the Anglican and Congregational establishments, which shouldered that responsibility in all but a few of the thirteen original colonies.

In the New Deal view, people in Maine and California were "neighbors." Ditto for New Yorkers and Texans. "Community" would now be understood nationally, and social well-being would be a national concern.

But the more significant departure may have been in the religious subtext implied in the New Deal's construction of the concept of community. In moving toward a *gracious* society cast in the image of a gracious God, the New Deal was departing from the *judging* society cast in the image of the judging (and often angry) God of Puritanism and Reformed Protestantism.

The 1996 legislation that dismantled a key component of the Social Security Act was entitled "The Personal Responsibility Act." In its own succinct way, the title belies the extent to which concepts of sin and merit, as opposed to grace, have come to permeate contemporary political discourse. It also exposes popular American beliefs about the nature and causes of poverty.

The youngest person to cast a ballot for Franklin Delano Roosevelt is now 86 years old. In less time than we realize, the living memory of a more generous mode of political discourse will have vanished from our society. By exploring the religious heritage of the New Deal, we gain a window into the values and worldviews that lay behind the reasoning and the rhetoric.

Doing so has the potential to provide critical illumination of contemporary patterns of discourse and to aid in the development of alternatives. It will also provide answers to some questions that continue to dog serious students of the New Deal. As recently as 1998, a gathering of 130 scholars at the FDR Library in Hyde Park, New York, expressed frustration in attempting to assess the influence of Catholic social teaching on the New Deal, despite the fact that FDR himself quoted a papal encyclical in one of his campaign speeches.

Had Frances Perkins been there, she could have answered their questions.

As the chief social policy advisor to the Democratic Party leader for twenty years, she more than anyone would be in a position to identify the sources of inspiration for the New Deal. But there is a more compelling reason. Perkins was a deeply religious person. She was an Anglo-Catholic, which is to say she was an Episcopalian who was drawn to the catholic heritage of the Church of England and its American daughter, the Episcopal Church. Throughout her twelve years in the New Deal, she spent one day a month in silent retreat at the Catonsville, Maryland, Convent of All Saints Sisters of the Poor, an Episcopal religious order. She was steeped in the writings of the British Anglo-Catholic socialists, in Thomas Aquinas, and the papal encyclicals.

For twenty years before she went to Washington, Perkins had been immersed in the unique religious culture of New York City, where high-church Anglicanism had played a formative role in shaping a public religious culture that was distinctly different from the idealist Protestantism that had long enjoyed national hegemony.

Tory in pedigree and catholic in theology, New York Anglicanism enjoyed religious precedency in a city where Roman Catholics and Jews tipped the balance in favor of a vision of community that was at once pluralistic and solidaristic. Together, these three groups forged a religious and civic culture that gave rise to what might be called a "politics of generosity." In 1932, this politics would move onto the national stage.

To fully appreciate just how different this New York religious culture was from the latter-day Puritanism that dominated the nineteenth century, it is necessary to return to an earlier time.

The year was 1891. The setting was old Trinity Church, sturdily enthroned on the highest point overlooking Wall Street. A processional cross led the choir and vested clergy down the center aisle. Processions themselves, especially those led by a cross, were rare enough in U.S. Protestantism in those days, but this one pushed the envelope beyond the latent fears of resurgent royalism that haunted nineteenth-century America. Behind the cross, a black man carried a *red* flag. This was *not* a liturgical banner of Pentecost, although Wellesley professor Vida Scudder assures us that the connection is clear.[1] No, this was *the* red flag, the one that would inspire—and terrify—the century to come.

Immediately behind him, a white man carried that other inspiring and terrifying flag—the "Stars 'n' Stripes." The occasion was the second in a series of Labor Sunday masses promoted by the Church Association for the Advancement of the Interests of Labor, popularly known by the acronym CAIL. Trade union officials marched in procession, and the rank and file filled the pews to overflowing, according to Scudder.

To those for whom the wealth and prestige of Trinity Church seemed to be its defining characteristics, this warm embrace of a social movement so offensive to the bourgeois sensibility must have seemed strange. What was at work here? Noblesse oblige? Paternalism? Appeasement of the restless masses? Veiled exploitation? Enlightened self-interest? Or radical chic?

Each theory has its apologists, but none would likely suggest that the alliance might have been based on a common worldview shaped by a common understanding of grace. In other words, no one would suggest that it might have been *theological.*

With the founding of the republic, New York State became the first North American polity to offer full citizenship to Jews.[2] By 1806, Roman Catholics enjoyed the same status. By the end of the nineteenth century, the majority of New York City residents would be Roman Catholic, with Jews and Episcopalians the second and third largest groups, respectively. All of the city's twentieth-century mayors would come from one of those three groups, as would most of the principals of the New Deal. (The quintessential mayoral example was Fiorello LaGuardia, an Episcopalian with a Catholic father and a Jewish mother.)

Although there is no evidence of an intentional effort to organize adherents of these three religious traditions into a political coalition, the fact is that they tended to function that way, and there was some recognition of that. For instance, it was common when some community initiative was in the formative stage for the leadership to say "We need someone from the Jewish community" or "We need a priest" to round out or enhance the credibility of the initiative. But there seems to be less awareness that commonalities in their religious backgrounds may partly explain why New Yorkers gravitated toward a "politics of generosity" rather than a "politics of righteousness," ultimately emphasizing social *provision* rather than social *discipline*.

In theological terms, it was the God of grace versus the God of judgment. In social terms, it was community as inherited relationship rather than community as voluntary association of the like-minded—the convinced and the converted. Philosophically, all three groups shared the Aristotelianism of the emerging social sciences rather than the Platonism of historic Protestantism, which is to say they were *realist* rather than *idealist*. All three tended to affirm the material and the existential, valuing relationships more than abstract principles, and tending to see human nature as basically good, with sin a forgivable consequence of human limitation rather than evidence of a pre-existing moral depravity. All three were racially, ethnically, and linguistically diverse. We can easily grasp the linguistic diversity of Catholic and Jewish immigrants, who came from many different countries. But even the Episcopal Diocese of New York could boast in 1900 that mass was celebrated every Sunday in nine different languages.

But to better understand the church that nurtured Perkins and the Roosevelts, let us momentarily return to those sign crimes in the 1891 Labor Sunday procession. What can we make of that curious juxtaposition of the "Stars 'n' Stripes" with the red flag of international socialism?"[3]

With similar reverence for the values of the state, this procession seemed to say that when socialism came to the United States, it would be red, but it would also be white and blue—constitutional, democratic, and *loyal*.

The cultural consistency is obvious. These Anglicans were heirs of a loyalist tradition—one that had a sacramental understanding of both *ecclesia* and *civitas*. The civil order was now a republic, but it was still an outward and visible sign of the grace God transmits through community. Can we be surprised that a church that valued civic and ecclesiastical unity so highly saw something sacramental in the "solidarity" the labor unions embodied?

The message was also theologically consistent. The material needs of human beings needed to be integrated into the framework of abstract ideas that governed the republic. Just as the Gospel of John suggested that the Word, in order to be fully understood, had to become Flesh, abstract ideals such as freedom and opportunity had to manifest themselves concretely in food, shelter, and adequate income—or they were just words. Can we be surprised to find this Johannine theology in a diocese that dedicated its cathedral to St. John the Divine? And can we see why it might have been agreeable to Roman Catholics, whose church at that time had twenty-two popes named John and only five named Paul?

And are we surprised to learn that during his presidency, one of New York's landed gentry, Franklin Roosevelt, would propose an economic bill of rights to balance the political Bill of Rights attached to the U.S. Constitution? Although it never became law in the United States, Eleanor Roosevelt, the First Lady turned global community-maker, would assure its inclusion in the Universal Declaration of Human Rights.

It was into *this* strain of loyalist, materialist, realist Anglicanism that Franklin and Eleanor Roosevelt were born, and it was to *this* Anglicanism that a 24-year-old Frances Perkins would make a lifelong commitment.

Born in 1880, and descended from Revolutionary War hero James Otis, little Fannie Coralie Perkins was of solid Yankee stock, baptized in the Plymouth Congregational Church in Worcester, Massachusetts. While a student at Mt. Holyoke, where she studied the natural sciences, Perkins was deeply influenced by the social justice classic, *How the Other Half Lives* by Jacob Riis, another New York Episcopalian, who would later serve the church as a member of its national Commission on the Relations of Capital and Labor. She was moved to action when the dynamic Florence Kelley of the National Consumers League lectured at the college.

Then a course with Professor Annah May Soule sent Perkins and her classmates into the factories of Holyoke to make surveys of working conditions. Perkins's biographer George Martin said the course gave Perkins "the opportunity to use her scientific training to test and build conclusions in a humanistic field. She discovered that one serious accident—say the loss of a man's hand—could drive a steady, sober working family into penury. Factory work, she learned, was so irregular that savings were continually exhausted. Avoiding poverty therefore was not only a question of simply liquor or laziness but also of safety devices on machines and of regularity of employment."[4]

Is it any wonder Perkins lost patience with those religious perspectives that emphasized personal responsibility and moral improvement when the problems so often were mechanical or systemic? Her enthusiasm for the laboratory and the field investigation may also have fostered a desire for the more experiential approach to truth found in liturgical traditions rich in art, drama, and nature imagery.

Fannie Perkins was determined to go into social work when she graduated from Mt. Holyoke, but necessity required her to take a series of teaching jobs, the last being at Ferry Hall in staunchly Presbyterian Lake Forest, Illinois. She began working weekends at Hull House, the famous Chicago settlement founded by Jane Addams and the devout Anglo-Catholic, Ellen Gates Starr. Although usually cited as an example of Protestant voluntarism, Hull House was actually modeled on Toynbee Hall, a Church of England mission that embodied the state church tradition to which the Episcopal Church was heir.

In the spring of 1905, Perkins resolved the other part of her dilemma by presenting herself for confirmation at the Church of the Holy Spirit, then a fledgling Anglo-Catholic beacon in Lake Forest. Following ancient Catholic practice, she took a new name at confirmation and would henceforth be known to the world as Frances Perkins.

These efforts apparently did the trick. By the fall of 1907, Perkins was on the trajectory that would guide the rest of her life—working for social justice in close association with the Episcopal Church. As executive secretary of the Philadelphia Research and Protective Association, an interfaith venture incubated by the Diocese of Pennsylvania, she obtained passage of landmark legislation regulating rooming houses.

Evidence suggests that Perkins worshipped at St. Clement's, another Anglo-Catholic beacon, and may have begun her lifelong relationship with All Saints Sisters of the Poor at that time.[5] The order had a team of sisters working in the parish, and they founded a hospital located directly across the street from the church. The building, today, is a dormitory for Moore College of Art and Design.

Although Perkins was in Philadelphia for only two years, she was very busy. She joined the Socialist Party and taught classes in sociology and economics at the diocesan headquarters while taking courses at the University of Pennsylvania under the legendary social work theorist, Simon Patten.

On his recommendation, she went to New York in 1909, to pursue a master's in political science at Columbia University. Columbia's president from 1902 to 1948 was the prominent churchman, Nicholas Murray Butler. Butler was FDR's colleague on the boards of trustees of both the cathedral and St. Stephen's (now Bard) College.[6] In 1931, he would share the Nobel Peace Prize with Jane Addams.

While at Columbia, Perkins resided at Greenwich House, a settlement headed by Mary Kingsbury Simkhovitch. Like Perkins, Simkhovitch had been raised a New England Congregationalist but had converted to Anglo-Catholicism when she was in college. She was also schooled in socialist thought, having attended the Second International in 1889. Her husband, Vladimir Simkhovitch, was a professor at Columbia and a convert to Anglo-Catholicism.

Mary Simkhovitch was also a close associate of the Rev. Charles K. Gilbert, who staffed the diocesan Social Service Commission, which led the Episcopal Church nationally in the development of legislative programs in housing, child welfare, and labor issues.[7] It would be Gilbert's counsel Perkins would seek twenty-three years later when she would be offered the appointment in the Presidential Cabinet. Gilbert told her he believed it was "God's own call."[8]

Upon graduation from Columbia, Perkins was hired by the National Consumers League and became their chief lobbyist in Albany, where she was instrumental in obtaining passage of the 54 Hour bill, a landmark piece of labor legislation prohibiting women of any age and boys under 18 from working more than 54 hours in a single week.

Then on a fateful Saturday afternoon in 1911, Perkins was having tea with a friend near Washington Square when they heard the clamor of horse-drawn fire trucks rushing to the east side of the square. The eighth, ninth, and tenth floors of the Asch Building were ablaze. The floors were home to the Triangle Shirtwaist Company, manufacturers of the famous "Gibson Girl" blouses. Despite eight fires in nine years of operation, the owners had refused to hold fire drills. Successful in their efforts to defeat unionization, some of the doors were kept locked to keep workers in and organizers out.

Now the Triangle Company was on fire again—for the last time. In all, 146 died and an untold number were injured. Forty-seven workers, some with flaming hair and clothing, jumped from the windows. Firemen tried to break their fall with nets and blankets, but the bodies hit with such force that the firemen somersaulted, the horses stampeded, and bodies crashed right through the sidewalks.

"The New Deal was born on March 25, 1911," Perkins would later say.

An outraged citizenry formed the Committee on Safety. With the blessing of the Consumer's League, Perkins accepted an assignment as the executive secretary. The Committee, in turn, "lent" her to the state legislature's newly created Factory Investigating Commission, organized by Al Smith.

In this work, her belief in experiential learning and her preference for liturgy combined. *Preaching to the legislators about the problem* was not enough. She would take these overweight, cigar-chomping politicians on surprise visits to factories at five o'clock in the morning, usher them over to the window, and point to the ice-covered wooden ladder propped against the wall, and say, "There, gentlemen. That's your fire escape." And out the window and down the slippery ladder they went.[9]

The result was that New York State, which accounted for one-third of the Gross National Product at this time, also led the nation in factory safety legislation.

She got away with these exercises, she later said, because she had learned early on that her trademark tricorn hat reminded these men of their mothers. (This "liturgy" included vestments!) As she put it, "I said to myself, 'That's the way to get things done. So behave, so dress, so comport yourself that you subconsciously remind them of their mothers.'"

When Al Smith was elected governor in 1918, it was Perkins who was in for a surprise. He told her he wanted to appoint her to the Industrial Commission, the agency that preceded the formation of the state Department of Labor. She felt that she was called to be a public advocate, not a public official, but Smith persuaded her that good people had to take responsibility for change. They could not just advocate it from afar. In other words, don't just preach the word. Embody it.

Perkins had also become a student of the social encyclicals emanating from the papacy, beginning with *Rerum Novarum* in 1891, which had endorsed the trade union movement. During the 1920s, she toured New York State with a Roman Catholic priest in an effort to educate the public about the content of these encyclicals.

When FDR was elected governor in 1928, he appointed Perkins to head the state labor department. As part of her work, she went to England twice to study the English unemployment insurance system, managing to squeeze in sessions at Maurice Reckitt's Anglo-Catholic Summer School of Christian Sociology, publishers of the socialist journal *Christendom*, where she studied with the likes of William Temple, R.H. Tawney, T.S. Eliot, and Dorothy Sayers.

When Roosevelt was elected President in 1932, Perkins would have the opportunity to translate much of this British social theory into U.S. policy. All social policy came under the purview of the Labor Department because there was no other place to put it. The Department of Health, Education, and Welfare and its two current successors, Health and Human Services, and Education, did not exist at the time and were created later, as spinoffs to programs initiated in the Labor Department. In other words, today, not just the Labor Department but also the Departments of Education and of Health and Human Services still bear Frances Perkins's imprint.

But it was not just social and labor policy where Perkins and the trappings of New York religious culture made themselves felt. Consider the types of programs the New Deal created: the federal projects for artists, writers, and theater (Boston still had official censorship of the theater at this time); the archiving of church records (including New York's diocesan archives); the development of the Soundex system to aid genealogical research through the U.S. Census.

And consider also the content of some of these programs. The Federal Theatre Project's first major success was, of all things, *Murder in the Cathedral*, T.S. Eliot's story of the martyrdom of Thomas à Becket, the beloved Archbishop of Canterbury, a story with unique appeal for both Anglicans and Roman Catholics.

Perkins also had a tendency to speak in terms of relationships, rather than moral principle, even when she agreed with the moral principle. In defending the decision to allow Emma Goldman to return to the United States, Perkins did not cite free speech, even though she was a strong civil libertarian. Instead, she said, "She's an old woman who just wants to see her friends again before she dies. Can't we allow her that?"

In a similar vein, when the CEO of General Motors appeared in her office with his top labor policy advisors to demand that the federal government send in troops to end the sit-down strike, Perkins said, "Look, you're the one who wants these people to work for you. They've told you they don't want to work for you on the terms you offer. So go talk to them. Find out what they want, and see if you can't offer them something that's going to make them want to work for you."

The policy advisors insisted there was a vital principle at stake, but she continued to discuss it in terms of relationships. They said, in effect, the government should punish disobedience, and she said, in effect, the government should encourage reconciliation. Perkins said the policy experts became ever more abstruse in their theories until the CEO finally stood up and said, "I want to go back to Detroit and make automobiles. I can make automobiles under any kind of labor policy!"

She attributed this outcome to *his* realism. Others would have attributed it to *her* tenacity. I once heard another biographer of Perkins liken her to a dog that gets hold of your ankle and just will not let go. In her own view, though, she was most likely just following the advice she gave her classmates at Mt. Holyoke in their final meeting before graduation, when she quoted St. Paul's text in 1 Corinthians, " . . . be ye steadfast, unmovable, always abounding in the work of the Lord . . . " The class chose "Be ye steadfast" as its motto.

Perkins always insisted there was no guiding ideology to the New Deal. As she saw it, they were just decent people trying to do the right thing, pretty much making it up as they went along. Mother Catherine Grace, one-time Superior of All Saints Sisters of the Poor, saw the hand of God in all that "making it up as they went along." She put it this way: "The Divine Architect used this soul mightily. Frances Perkins was a sensitive instrument in His hands. She listened, she heard, and she executed. Through this attentiveness, the Social Security Act came to fruition."

MY MATERNAL grandparents retired without Social Security. My grandfather had cancer and was an invalid— eventually a bed patient. They survived economically by having one of their children, usually with a spouse and sometimes other family members, live with them for a while. This setup would pay the rent and keep groceries on the table, but it was not always a happy situation. Usually, everyone was living in a couple of rented rooms in a house.

My father was a logger, and my mother did seasonal work in the pepper plant in Woodbury, Georgia, paying in enough quarters to be eligible for Social Security. In retirement, they generally lived in subsidized housing and had enough money from their Social Security to pay rent and pay for utilities, food, and a few extras.

The important thing with Social Security is that, with the government controlling it, it is a guaranteed income. Many people, including many in my own family, if they had to invest part of their income for retirement, would retire having nothing on which to live.

— WALTER SKINNER —
MORELAND, GEORGIA

New Deal Warriors

June Hopkins

When June Hopkins, who held a Master's Degree
in Public Administration, became interested in
investigating the life and social work career of her
grandfather, Harry Hopkins, she returned to academia
and earned a Master's Degree, and then a Ph.D., in
history. Hopkins now heads the history department
at Armstrong Atlantic State University, a position she
has held for six years. Her book, *Harry Hopkins: Sudden
Hero, Brash Reformer*, was published in 1999 and *Jewish
First Wife, Divorced: The Correspondence of Ethel Gross
and Harry Hopkins*, co-edited with her daughter Allison
Giffen, came out in 2002. It is significant that for her
grandmother, Ethel Gross Hopkins Conant, Social
Security became a crucial means of support until she
died in 1976 at the age of 90.

*W*hen Franklin Roosevelt took the oath of office as President of the United States in early March of 1933, as many as 25 percent of American workers were unemployed and impoverished as a result of the economic catastrophe known as the Great Depression. Failed businesses dumped more workers onto the streets; failed banks eliminated life savings in a day. In response, the President and his New Dealers established an unprecedented array of programs, dubbed "Alphabet Agencies," to address these serious problems that seemed to threaten our democracy.

The most pressing problem was finding work for the able-bodied unemployed. Convinced that the country's economy could not hope to recover unless idle workers found jobs, Secretary of Labor Frances Perkins and Federal Relief Administrator Harry Hopkins took the lead in many of the Administration's efforts to put Americans back to work. Both of these influential social reformers had been active in the progressive movement that emerged during the early part of the twentieth century and was especially strong in New York City.

Perkins had been involved in social reform since she graduated from Mount Holyoke in 1902, but her reforming instincts rose to new heights after she witnessed the Triangle Shirtwaist Factory Fire in March of 1911. After graduating from Grinnell College in Iowa in 1912, Hopkins arrived in New York City to work in a settlement house on the Lower East Side and from there became a locally prominent social worker. Their paths first crossed at that time. Almost two decades later, these two dynamos worked closely together again in Albany as members of Governor Franklin Roosevelt's two administrations during the early years of the Depression.

Then, in 1932, their boss ran successfully for President of the United States. Just after his inauguration in 1933, FDR brought first Perkins and then Hopkins to Washington. Both became part of his inner White House circle. They brought with them the belief that the federal government had both the power and the duty to ensure the welfare of all citizens. This was consonant with the President's mindset. Given the dire economic conditions, businesses could not afford to absorb these unemployed workers. The government had to act. First, Congress passed laws to allow the government to provide direct relief to destitute Americans. This agency, the Federal Emergency Relief Administration (FERA), was unprecedented; the need was great and the need was immediate. People were starving in America.

Perkins and Hopkins were not political radicals but both believed, along with the President, that this direct relief, the dole, while perhaps necessary for the short term, was humiliating. The American worker wanted and deserved, most of all, to work for a secure wage. So, the federal government, through FERA, sponsored work relief programs and created public jobs for unemployed workers on relief. These workers on government projects received wages that were equal to their relief payments. This too was unprecedented. But the two reformers were willing to cut a new path in order to see that the American people were helped. After all, in his inaugural address, the President had promised action on the part of the government in order to allay the fear that was gripping the nation.

In the summer of 1934—four long years into the Great Depression—a vast army of unemployed and idle workers still existed.

Three-and-a-half million able-bodied Americans were on relief. Precious skills were being lost. For the President, this was an untenable situation. The President also knew that in a modern industrial, capitalist nation, there would be inevitable booms and busts that would result in further unemployment and increased poverty. Only the power of the federal government could protect its citizens when a bust occurred.

As a consequence, FDR established a Committee for Economic Security (CES), consisting of Hopkins, Secretary of the Treasury Henry Morgenthau, Jr., Secretary of Agriculture Henry Wallace, Attorney General Homer Cummings, and Perkins, the first female Cabinet member, whom he named chair. He charged the committee to create comprehensive legislation to protect Americans against insecurity and distress due to "the hazards and vicissitudes of modern life," including unemployment, accident, sickness, invalidity, old age, and premature death. In his letter of transmittal to the committee members, the President wrote that an economic security program "must have as its primary aim the assurance of an adequate income to each human being in childhood, youth, middle age, or old age—in sickness and in health." The legislation would provide cradle-to-grave economic safeguards for all Americans. Perkins pushed for unemployment insurance and old age pensions, and Hopkins hoped to have a permanent government jobs program included in the bill.

The Roosevelt Administration was certainly picking its way over new ground, but any fears that the new policy would be radical were soon laid to rest. When Roosevelt created the CES, he declared: "Our task of reconstruction does not require the creation of new and strange values. It is rather the finding of the way once more to known, but to some degree forgotten, ideals and values. If the means and the details are in some instances new, the objectives are as permanent as human nature."

Hopkins also felt a strong affinity to such traditional values as democracy and the self-reliance of the American worker within the capitalist system. Roosevelt sent Hopkins on a trip to Europe and England in the summer of 1934 to assess alternative ways of dealing with the economic ills brought by the Great Depression, which was worldwide. Hopkins concluded that the United States had to adopt a recovery program tailored to the nation's specific situation. He declared that while the English system of relief was indeed impressive, it could not be "transplanted." The United States must develop its own program with two distinct policy branches—one ensuring the delivery of social insurance and the other assuring workers of a job. During a press conference in London, Hopkins announced that President Roosevelt would soon introduce a broad plan of Social Security to the American public, one that would encompass "all the rights of a civilized people," including a federally guaranteed assurance of a job for all able-bodied workers. In Hopkins's mind, unemployment relief and job assurance had to be integrated into the President's plan for economic recovery. Old age pensions would take care of the elderly, eventually; aid to dependent children would take care of the very young. Neither of these groups was expected to work.

Thus, with jobs assured for all who could work, recovery would trickle up from the increased buying power of the newly employed rather than trickle down from increased prices and government support for business. To Hopkins, jobs and wages for the unemployed seemed the most effective way to preserve the traditional American values of independence and self-sufficiency and the most direct road to full economic health for the nation.

Hopkins drew from the past to justify the innovative methods of the New Deal, but he made no secret of his attachment to the somewhat radical idea of a permanent federal work enterprise to cope with the cyclical unemployment inherent in a capitalist, democratic nation. Because of Hopkins's influence with the President, many thought that this was a definite possibility.

He told FDR that the unemployed had little hope of finding jobs in private industry. He argued that unemployment insurance and old age pensions were insufficient guards against economic insecurity, and that some "established practices" would have to be rearranged. Government work projects would stimulate the economy through public money, which would be spent for materials to support these projects and then re-spent by newly confident, wage-earning workers. Government jobs would prime the economic pump. And this, Hopkins declared, "is as American as corn on the cob."

Unemployment relief, whatever form it might take, was central to President Roosevelt's overall plan for economic security. "Fear and worry," the President declared, "based on unknown danger contribute to social unrest and economic demoralization. If, as our constitution tells, our federal government was established among other things, 'to promote the general welfare,' it is our plain duty to provide for that security upon which welfare depends. I stand or fall by my refusal to accept as a necessary condition of our future, a permanent army of unemployed."

In September of 1934, Hopkins had every reason to believe that public employment would be part of the proposed legislation. He and his staff drew up a "Plan to Give Work to the Able-Bodied Needy Unemployed," which outlined ways to put people to work on government-sponsored projects. Work relief—the previous policy of working off cash assistance under the FERA—was only "a stepping stone to the new Works Program [which would provide] full-time work, assurance of earnings, and continuity of employment." It would not be merely an emergency measure. It would be a permanent government program that would ensure that heads of households remain breadwinners for their families. Furthermore, this proposed Works Program would provide help for a large group of already unemployed workers (about 16.8 million) who would not be eligible for unemployment insurance benefits. Yet what Hopkins had hoped would become the permanent third instrument of government relief policy never materialized.

Roosevelt wanted a draft of the Economic Security bill by December 15, 1934, and the completed bill on his desk by January, when the new Congress reconvened. This was not a great deal of time for such a mammoth undertaking. The CES had been delayed in getting started; both Perkins and Hopkins had been traveling and the committee did not get up to speed until September. Assisted by the Advisory Council on Economic Security and a Technical Board, the CES debated old age pensions, unemployment insurance, and aid to dependent children. Members also debated Hopkins's suggestion for a permanent federal jobs program. However, this portion of the original Economic Security bill never made it through to the floor of Congress. The Advisory Committee worried that a government employment program would be virtually indistinguishable from relief; it would also be enormously expensive. Although the CES did recommend that the government should employ workers that American industry could not support, the permanent federal work program was not part of the Economic Security bill. Instead, Congress passed the Emergency Relief Appropriation Act of 1935, which established the very important, but temporary, Works Progress Administration (WPA). FDR named Hopkins head of this agency that provided jobs for millions of idle Americans from 1935 to 1942.

Although the Social Security Act, which the Economic Security bill came to be known, did establish federal responsibility for the welfare of Americans through old age pensions, unemployment insurance, and aid to dependent children, it did not create the welfare system that Hopkins had envisioned. A federal guarantee of a regular income for a minimum standard of living earned through the dignity of a job remains an unfinished task.

MY STEPFATHER, Thomas B. Cahill, was a conductor on the New York Central Railroad. Franklin Roosevelt traveled on his train when he was going home to Hyde Park. One day the President called Tom into his compartment. He told Tom that he was contemplating instituting a retirement insurance program for workers, and he wanted to begin with railroad workers as a kind of experiment. He asked Tom what kind of program would be helpful to railroad workers after they could no longer work. I don't know what Tom told him, but subsequently the Railroad Retirement Act was passed, the forerunner of the Social Security Act.

— HOPE C. BOGORAD —
WASHINGTON, DC

Frances Perkins Conceives a Plan

KIRSTIN DOWNEY

Kirstin Downey, an economics reporter at the
Washington Post from 1988 to 2008, is the author of
*The Woman Behind The New Deal: The Life and Legacy of
Frances Perkins—Social Security, Unemployment Insurance,
and the Minimum Wage.* She was a writer and investigator
for the Financial Crisis Inquiry Commission, which
completed a book-length report on the causes of the
mortgage meltdown. Seven of her family members,
including three grandparents, three aunts, and her
mother, have received or are receiving Social Security.
For four of them, as a result of divorce, bad luck, or
poor investments, it ended up being their only source
of income in retirement. This is not that unusual: For
nearly 30 percent of American women older than 75,
Social Security is their only source of income.

*T*he Great Depression exposed weaknesses at the core of the nation's economic system. Then, as now, few of the nation's seniors had made adequate provision for their golden years. Even those with savings saw their hard-earned dollars dissipate in failed stock and real estate investments, sometimes in minutes. The boom and bust cycle of capitalism can be merciless to those who find themselves on the wrong side of the market without time to recover.

The pension system, then as now, provided inadequate shelter. Of some 6.5 million senior citizens in the United States at the time, only about 300,000 had public pensions, through state or federal retirement systems. Another 150,000 received pensions from their private employers or unions. The rest were on their own.

Older people flooded into the workforce, and soon more than a quarter of Americans were out of work. Once employers had their pick of workers, age discrimination, a deep-rooted problem in a youth-crazed culture, reared its ugly head. People 60 and over became virtually unemployable; their work skills came to be viewed as outdated and obsolete. Some 30 percent to 50 percent of the elderly sought support from friends or relatives. Adult children often found the burden unendurable. Humiliated seniors turned to charity, and around 700,000 obtained federal relief. It was a crisis.

Frances Perkins, the new Secretary of Labor under President Franklin Delano Roosevelt, had been turning this question over in her mind all her adult life. The answer, she had decided, had to be an old age pension of some kind, perhaps something like they had had in Europe for decades.

She knew it would need to be handled differently. In other countries, while employees and employers contributed to the pension system, the central governments also made significant contributions from general funds. In the United States it would be difficult, if not impossible, to convince citizens that the government should become the primary supporter of people's elderly years. She focused on ensuring that people could contribute substantially to their own accounts, thus lessening the government's burden. She looked to the insurance model, in which people pay in when they are employed, so that they can get money back when they are not.

She nagged President Franklin Delano Roosevelt, a pragmatic and charismatic politician, to give it consideration and push it forward. "It is probably our only chance in twenty-five years to get a bill like this," she told Roosevelt.

Finally, Roosevelt gave her the nod. With joblessness rampant, Frances decided to go for unemployment insurance first. If such a program went through smoothly, then perhaps old age insurance could be next. She was uncertain about the outcome. Even the piece that seemed the most likely to pass—unemployment insurance—seemed radical to many Americans. Few employers supported the idea. Some scholars had written books about it and Wisconsin had enacted its own state version, but the concept was still widely ridiculed. Just a few years earlier, Thomas Eliot later recalled, he had attended a play in which cartoonish characters walked onstage carrying placards reading "We Want Unemployment Insurance," which, he recalled, drew a "big laugh from the audience."

U.S. Representative David Lewis, a former coal miner from

Cumberland, Maryland, took the lead and introduced an employment compensation bill written by Eliot, who was assistant solicitor in the Labor Department, under Perkins's direction. The House Ways and Means Committee held hearings on it in March of 1934. Frances testified in support, and the bill seemed likely to sail toward easy approval.

But suddenly, Roosevelt held back. He decided to delay, because he was beginning to think the time was ripe for a program far more sweeping than just the unemployment insurance bill. Instead they would initiate a much more expansive "economic security" program that would cover people from cradle to grave. The concept included not only unemployment insurance, which would tide over the jobless workers who were the primary source of support to children and old people, but also old age pensions, which would provide income to people when they were too old to work; health insurance, so people would have medical care, even when they had no money; and financial assistance for the handicapped and for widowed women with children. Many widowed women earned so little money that losing their husbands meant that they must put their youngsters to work or place them in orphanages.

To create an intellectual underpinning for the effort, Roosevelt and Perkins set up a Cabinet-level economic security committee to do the groundwork. They had shared a predilection for creating committees or boards to get things done ever since they had worked together in Albany, when Perkins had served as Roosevelt's Industrial Commissioner. She served on eighteen such committees during Roosevelt's presidency. Typically she closely managed the process. She would set the agenda for the outcome she wanted, and the President would lend his prestige to the effort by ceremoniously appointing the people Frances had picked. Roosevelt preferred work of this kind to be done with minimal publicity. When there was a big splash to be made, he would make it and take credit for it.

In the creation of this particular committee, Frances employed the tricks she had learned over a lifetime. Roosevelt named her as the chair. Frances drafted letters appointing the members, and then had FDR sign them. She chose the other members carefully: Harry Hopkins, who had become Federal Emergency Relief Administrator, Secretary of Agriculture Henry Wallace, by then her closest friend in the Cabinet, Treasury Secretary Henry Morgenthau, and Attorney General Homer Cummings. But not everyone was willing to work hard on an economic security program or was even that interested in it. Frances decided to make sure to hold the Cabinet members' feet to the fire. In a meeting with Roosevelt present, she went around the table and extracted from each of the major members of her committee a pledge to support the program being prepared by the committee. Publicly obligated, they could not back down later.

On June 8, 1934, Roosevelt formally unveiled the plans. He said he intended to create a program that would provide "security against the hazards and vicissitudes of life." His plan would include both state and federal components, with funds raised by individual payroll contributions rather than from general taxes.

Then Frances looked for staff to implement the innovative program. She loaded the support staff with allies, including Labor Department official Arthur Altmeyer, and tapped a Wisconsinite, Edwin Witte, chairman of the University of Wisconsin economics department, as executive director. But Roosevelt had allotted no money to launch even the study group. Frances went hat in hand to raise money and borrow staff from other departments. The Federal Emergency Relief Administration, under Hopkins, came up with an initial $87,500 and then another $57,000.

Assembling a staff of qualified technical experts proved unexpectedly difficult, particularly considering the high unemployment rate among academics and professionals. Some social insurance experts, in particular I. M. Rubinow and Abraham Epstein, were brilliant specialists but also argumentative and publicly feuded with each other. They were not asked to participate, and they felt slighted. Other people accepted offers but had previous obligations that prevented them from starting right away. Some academics eagerly wrote reports but lacked good sense about what might be politically feasible. Despite the challenges, a core of specialized academic experts began working in concert on the program within a few months.

Constitutional issues were delegated to the twenty-six-year-old Labor Department's assistant solicitor Eliot. It was a difficult job: The Supreme Court was politically conservative and typically issued hostile decisions about humanitarian regulations. A group of four hostile Supreme Court justices—McReynolds, Butler, Van Devanter, and Sutherland, with occasional support from Roberts and Chief Justice Hughes—were known as the "battalion of death" for worker-friendly legislation. Unemployment insurance and old age pensions looked especially vulnerable to judicial attack.

Two other Supreme Court justices, however, provided crucial guidance behind the scenes. Elizabeth Brandeis Raushenbush, a young economist living in Wisconsin who was a social insurance advocate, discussed the problem with her father, Justice Louis Brandeis. She asked her father if he had any ideas about legal approaches that could put such a measure on solid constitutional grounds. Brandeis, speaking theoretically, suggested a plan in which contributions to state unemployment reserves could be offset against federal payroll taxes, thus avoiding any problematic direct federal contributions for this purpose. Brandeis's daughter told Frances Perkins about the idea at a holiday dinner party on New Year's Day.

Meanwhile, Justice Harlan F. Stone had whispered some words of advice as well. At an afternoon party at Stone's home, Frances was drinking tea with the justice when he asked her how things were going. She told him they were wrestling with how to establish an economic security program. Stone looked around to see if anyone was listening, then leaned in toward Frances. "The taxing power, my dear, the taxing power," he said in quiet tones.

The Labor Department soon drafted a measure along the lines laid out by Brandeis and Stone. But the job proved immense. The Cabinet committee found itself stymied by the magnitude of the tasks and the difficulty in deciding how to administer these new programs. The Cabinet committee met once a week through the fall. Only Frances attended all the meetings, although Hopkins, Morgenthau, and Wallace were there frequently as well. Some members barely attended at all, simply sending delegates in their places. Frances kept pushing, however.

Roosevelt had set an arbitrary Christmas deadline for completing the committee's work, but as the holiday approached, many details were unresolved. On the night of December 22 or 23, committee leaders were called to the Georgetown house—a rented house at 3304 O Street NW—where Frances was living. She led them into the dining room, placed a large bottle of Scotch on the table, and told them no one would leave until the work was done. Suitably fortified against the winter chill, they rolled up their sleeves and set to work.

On December 24, just barely meeting the presidential deadline, she and Hopkins presented the committee's findings and recommendations to Roosevelt. He accepted them, saying he would promptly send a message to Congress. Then new opposition sprang up from various corners over various provisions. Agriculture Department officials said it was too restrictive and failed to provide generously enough for workers. Treasury Department conservatives criticized its expenditures and the risk of "alarming business"; while liberals asserted the provisions were so weak they had "little value." Frances had to fend off detractors from both departments, by leaning on their bosses, Henry Wallace and Henry Morgenthau, and making some last-minute changes that won their support.

After that, the committee released a unanimous report.

On January 17, 1935, about ten months after the process had begun, Roosevelt urged passage of the Economic Security legislation. At first all went well. But then reporters interviewed the experts from the advisory council, outside advisors, and support staff, all eager to expound on their dissenting views. Many newspapers counseled a delay, saying more time was required to consider the provisions more carefully and build political support.

Fueled by negative press reports, Congress reacted with hostility to some of the proposed legislation, and opposition began to grow. Witte quickly saw the wisdom of the President's plan to keep all the program components together, for while the old age pension system would likely have been enacted by this time, the other parts of the program would surely have fallen by the wayside. Eliot boosted the entire package's chances by flipping the elements of the bill. He placed old age insurance as the front section in the legislation, which "had the effect of drawing away opposition from the other titles, which had much less popular support."

Congressional hearings were set for January 22. Witte and Perkins testified in support of the bill. Frances also explained how age discrimination made it essential to provide a benefit to people whom employers did not want to hire, making Social Security a vital part of reducing unemployment in America and also increasing opportunities for younger workers.

Witnesses lined up to discuss the bill. Academics and theoreticians who had long advocated forms of Social Security spoke, but many were unsatisfied that the plans did not meet their personal visions.

Employer testimony was mixed. The National Association of Manufacturers vehemently attacked the bill, calling it the "ultimate socialistic control of life and industry." Henry I. Harriman, president of the U.S. Chamber of Commerce, suggested some amendments but generally favored it. Many businessmen, however, wrote to Congress saying that while they supported the concept, they rejected the proposed taxes.

The measure again looked like a failing proposition. Witte had come to the reluctant conclusion that few legislators actually wanted the bill but that they did not want to anger the President by expressing opposition publicly. A *New York Times* headline of March 30, 1935, said it all: "Hopes Are Fading for Security Bill."

Recognizing that the bill was at risk, Frances rushed to rally other supporters. She secured fifty signatures of prominent people in a letter urging prompt passage. Slowly the tide began to turn. A letter-writing campaign by Americans urging support for senior citizens made some legislators come to view the economic security measure as a more acceptable compromise than the more farfetched suggestions being proposed by their constituents.

Final passage in the House came on April 19, 1935, on a 10-to-1 vote margin, with one significant change. The Economic Security Act had become the Social Security Act, possibly because of the references to "social security" in a landmark book by Epstein. Ironically, while the term worldwide continued to refer to a comprehensive system of economic security programs—from maternity care to unemployment, welfare and old age pensions—in the United States, popular usage came to refer only to payments to the elderly.

Congressional opinion in the Senate seemed even more unreliable than in the House of Representatives. Members of the Senate Finance Committee, which handled the bill, were mostly conservative Southerners with high seniority. Ultimately, they approved the measure—with one important caveat. They added an amendment placing the Social Security Board, which would administer the old age and unemployment programs, inside the Labor Department but said that the Secretary of Labor should play no role in hiring its personnel. Her support for Social Security and other humanitarian ventures had allowed her to be painted as dangerously subversive, a label that would haunt her for the rest of her life. Then the new agency was pulled entirely from her oversight and made an independent office. In the end, the Senate passed the bill overwhelmingly.

The old age insurance program was initially more limited in scope than it is today. Agricultural and domestic workers were exempted, against Frances's wishes, because Treasury officials said collecting their taxes would prove overly difficult. Therefore, blacks and Hispanics, who were more likely to be farm workers or domestic servants, were disproportionately excluded, even though most earned such low wages that Social Security would have been their only source of retirement income.

Low-wage church employees, such as secretaries and janitors, also found themselves without retirement assistance. Church officials had obtained exemption for their employees, partially because retired clergymen mistakenly believed they would lose their church pensions if they were included in Social Security.

Congress, meanwhile, created new problems by underfunding the Social Security trust fund. Workers initially paid in at a rate of a one percent tax on employers and one percent on employees, but the rate was supposed to be gradually raised to 3 percent by 1949. However, Congress had no appetite for raising taxes even slightly, although their calculations said it would be necessary. Consequently, within a few decades, large shortfalls in the program's funding emerged.

On August 14, 1935, the President signed the measure into law, and the Social Security Act became effective immediately. FDR said it had been constructed in a way that no future politician would be able to tinker with it, because it had been funded by workers' own contributions.

Frances echoed this assessment: "One thing I know: Social Security is so firmly embedded in the American psychology today that no politician, no political party, no political group could possibly destroy this Act and still maintain our Democratic system," she told the staff of the Social Security Administration in 1962.

The "New Deal's Most Important Act," proclaimed *The Washington Post* that day. "Its importance cannot be exaggerated . . . because this legislation eventually will affect the lives of every man, woman, and child in the country."

Many people would later claim credit for the creation of Social Security, but to those closest to the process, Frances was most responsible.

"The one person, in my opinion, above all others who was responsible for there being a Social Security program in the early 1930s was Frances Perkins," said Maurine Mulliner, an assistant to Senator Robert Wagner, who left his office to join the Social Security Board soon after it was created. "I don't think that President Roosevelt had the remotest interest in a Social Security bill or program. He was simply pacifying Frances."

"She deserved much of the credit for getting this legislation through," said Marion B. Folsom, an executive at Eastman Kodak, who had represented business interests during the deliberations over the bill.

Perkins said that Social Security was a direct result of the downward spiral of economic events that started in the 1920s. "Nothing else would have bumped the American people into Social Security except something so shocking, so terrifying, as that depression," she said later.

On the day the bill was signed, Perkins issued a statement hailing "one of the most forward-looking pieces of legislation in the interest of wage earners" in history.

In public, she hid her feelings of disappointment about being blocked from administrative control of the agency and never blamed anyone but herself for that decision. She ended up naming most of its top officials, who were appointed by the President.

By 1936, Frances reported that nearly 1 million people were receiving benefits. Nearly three-quarters of a million were old people, 184,000 were dependent children, and nearly 18,000 were blind. She also said that all the states were now enacting unemployment compensation laws, including fifteen that had done so since the Social Security Act was passed.

She had changed America forever.

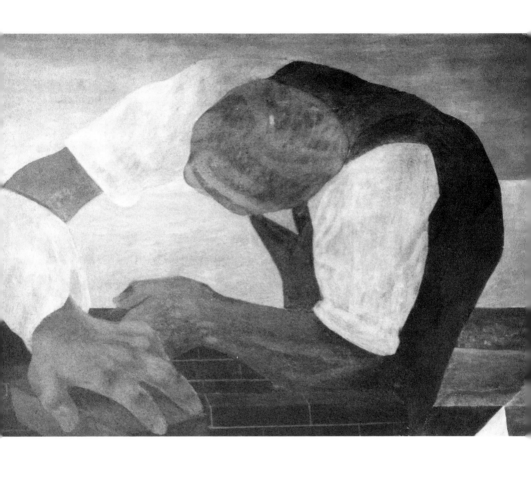

MY MOTHER passed away when I was six years old, leaving my father to care for six children ranging in age from 6 to 16. He worked very hard to provide for us and to keep our family together, which was difficult, as being a single father was not common at the time. My two older brothers also worked to contribute to the family expenses, as did my three older sisters when they were able. The youngest, I also began working when I was a teenager.

Often it felt like a battle. Are we going to be homeless? Are we going to be separated?

Social Security provided a critical bit of ammunition against poverty. The survivors benefits the six children received helped us deal with the realities of living in a month-to-month economic situation. The money provided from Social Security allowed my family to pay the rent and to eat—when otherwise it wouldn't have been possible.

My father had to be very open with us about the finances. There was no hiding our situation. As a family, we were very aware from where money came from—and went. So, from a very early age, I have understood the critical importance of Social Security for everyone.

Social Security allowed my family to pay the rent, to eat, and to stay together as a family.

— BRIAN LUNDQUIST —
SOUTH PORTLAND, MAINE

EDITORS' NOTE: The following letter from former Republican Governor of New Hampshire John Gilbert Winant to President Roosevelt, resigning as a member and chair of the three-member Social Security Board, which oversaw the implementation of Social Security, highlights the Republican attacks on FDR and Social Security in the 1936 presidential campaign. Breaking with his party to support FDR and defend Social Security in the campaign, Governor Winant played a key part in securing the new program and contributing to FDR's landslide victory. Frances Perkins had been the first to urge Roosevelt to appoint Winant to the Social Security Board and subsequently to make Winant head of the International Labor Organization in Geneva. This service was followed by Winant's becoming U.S. Ambassador to the Court of St. James in England from 1941 to 1946, again on the strong recommendation of Secretary Perkins. Recent analyses of Winant's extraordinary service can be found in Kirstin Downey's *The Woman Behind the New Deal* and Lynne Olson's *Citizens of London: The Americans Who Stood with Britain in Its Darkest, Finest Hour.*

SOCIAL SECURITY BOARD
WASHINGTON, D.C.

September 28, 1936

John G. Winant, Chairman
Arthur J. Altmeyer
Vincent M. Miles

My dear Mr. President,

On August 14, 1935, the Social Security Act became law. The administration of its major provisions was entrusted to a Board of three members. Under the law not more than two members of the Board could be "members of the same political party". You named me to the Board and as a Republican and as the minority member my appointment was confirmed by the Senate on August 23, 1935, together with the other two members, without objection.

It was clearly the intention of Congress to create a non-partisan Board, with personnel protected under Civil Service, and to insure non-partisan administration of the Act. It has been so administered.

The Act itself was viewed as a non-partisan humanitarian measure. Three times as many Republicans in Congress voted for the Social Security Act as voted against it.

Having seen the tragedy of war, I have been consistently interested in the ways of peace. Having seen some of the cruelties of the depression, I have wanted to help with others in lessening the hardships, the suffering, and the humiliations forced upon American citizens because of our precious failure as a nation to provide effective social machinery for meeting the problems of dependency and unemployment. The Social Security Act is America's answer to this great human need.

The references to the problems of social security in the platform of the Republican party were disappointing. It was my hope that the position of the Republican presidential nominee might be less so.

Today we know that both the Republican platform and the Republican candidate have definitely rejected the constructive provisions of the Social Security Act, only to fall back upon the dependency dole—a dole with a means test, which in my state includes the pauper's oath and disenfranchisement.

The statements that provisions of this Act are "a fraud on the working man" and "a cruel hoax" I believe are untrue. They are charges with regard to a measure which had the support of 372 members of the House of Representatives, as against the 33 opposed—which met with the approval of 77 members of the United States Senate with only six against—which was upheld by the votes of Senator Hiram Johnson, Senator LaFollette, Senator Costigan, Senator Wagner, and Representative David J. Lewis—a measure which was advocated by such advisers to the Committee on Economic Security as President Green of the American Federation of Labor, President Frank P. Graham of the University of North Carolina, Miss Grace Abbott, former Chief of the Children's Bureau, and Monsignor John A. Ryan of the National Catholic Welfare Conference.

I have never assumed that the Social Security Act was without fault. I had assumed and even hoped that time and experience might dictate many and important changes. As you stated when you signed the Act on August 14, 1935: "This law represents a cornerstone in a structure which is being built, but is by no means complete." But Governor Landon's address at Milwaukee on the Social Security Act was not a plea for the improvement of the Act; it was a plea to scrap the Act.

I am interested in the social security program not from a partisan viewpoint. I am interested in it as a humanitarian measure. Governor Landon has made the problem of social security a major issue in this campaign and I cannot support him. I do not feel that members of independent Commissions or Boards, such as the Social Security Board, should take an active part in politics and moreover, I was appointed and confirmed as the minority member. While I retain this position I am not free to defend the Act. Therefore, I am tending you my resignation as a member of the Social Security Board.

No work I have ever undertaken seemed more worthwhile to me than my brief service on the Social Security Board. May I thank you for the opportunity of this service and join you in defending it.

Sincerely,

[signed] John G. Winant

The President
The White House
Washington, D.C.

I'VE RECEIVED three blessings from Social Security. My grandfather lost his farm during the Great Depression and died of pneumonia due to exposure working on construction of the Roselawn Cemetery in Madison, Wisconsin. His compensation included two burial plots ensuring his resting place, but left his widow homeless.

My beloved Swedish grandmother moved in with us as a very unwelcome mother-in-law to my unhappy mother—a situation so universal that it was a staple for some comedians. She was given one of the first Social Security checks and turned it over to my parents. She kept house, allowing my estranged parents to work their 18 hour days in restaurants and spend their days off apart—he in a tavern—she in marathon double features at all the movie theaters. She taught me Swedish Graces as her namesake and I was ecstatic to accompany her on the only two movies she ever saw: Greta Garbo in "Queen Christina" and Walt Disney's "Sleeping Beauty." Life at home was good with school as my other sanctuary until I was 15. The headlines: "Hitler Invades Poland" didn't affect me, but

Grandma mourned, "*Ah hunsun, dat Hitler vants to rule da world.*" I am convinced that God spared her from the horrors of World War II by taking her before Pearl Harbor, while robbing me of my only mentor.

In 2001, when my husband died after 53 years of marriage, I had no earnings of my own as a stay-at-home wife and mother. The second blessing of the Social Security widow's pension shelters me from the humiliations and derision of the bad old days I remember.

In 2010, I celebrated its third blessing. My son David, who suffered from emphysema, slept sitting up in my front room for a year as he earned enough money for a used truck to get him to Montana and a cottage, promised for sweat equity. He soon collapsed and lingered near death for a month while I was powerless to help at age 86. He was awarded a Social Security disability pension based on unsuspected asbestosis from exposure 30 years ago. Now we both have peace of mind and he keeps his dignity facing a very limited future.

— Selma Calnan —
BISHOP, CALIFORNIA

Frances Perkins and the Administration of Social Security

Larry DeWitt

Larry DeWitt is the historian at the U. S. Social Security Administration and is the principal editor of *Social Security: A Documentary History*, published in 2008 by Congressional Quarterly Press. Larry's mother and several aunts and uncles depend on Social Security for the bulk of their retirement income. A few years ago, when his mother suffered a brain aneurysm while on an out-of-state vacation, she had to have emergency brain surgery and spent a month in the hospital under the care of a variety of specialists. Without her Medicare coverage, the resulting medical bills would have forced the family into bankruptcy. On a recent family vacation, Larry's uncle Jay—a World War II veteran—told him "Thank God for Social Security. I think it's probably the best thing the government has ever done."

*W*hen President Franklin Roosevelt asked Frances Perkins to become the first woman in American history to serve in a president's Cabinet as his Secretary of Labor, she initially resisted the idea. But when the President insisted he needed her, she consented to serve, but only if the President would commit to her ambitious agenda. Among other issues, she told FDR she would join his Cabinet only if he agreed to support unemployment and old age social insurance.

When it came time, in the summer of 1934, to address social insurance, the President created a Cabinet-level committee (the Committee on Economic Security, CES) to study the matter and develop the Administration's legislative proposals. He appointed Perkins as the chair of that committee. Perkins turned to her young Assistant Secretary of Labor, Arthur Altmeyer, and to a University of Wisconsin economist, Edwin Witte, to oversee the technical work required, while she and her Cabinet-level colleagues formulated the broad policy and political aspects of the effort.

Not only did Perkins oversee all the work of the CES with an indefatigable determination, she and Witte formed a kind of "tag team" on Capitol Hill, as the Administration's lead witnesses at the congressional hearings.

We might say that Franklin Roosevelt commissioned the structure, and that Frances Perkins was the architect of the Social Security program.

LOSING A BATTLE BUT WINNING THE WAR

"Administration is legislation in action," was the motto of the great Progressive-era economist John R. Commons, of the University of Wisconsin. Commons instilled this motto in his graduate students, several of whom would play prominent roles in the early administration of the new Social Security program. Altmeyer, one of his students, came to his role in Social Security through his association with Frances Perkins. The John Commons ethos was one both Altmeyer and Perkins shared.

Perkins understood the vital importance of an effective administrative launch of the system to its long-term success. She knew that creating a new social program, and getting it through the legislative process, while immense tasks, were only two-thirds of the job. Vitally important, too, was that the program be institutionalized in a way that would provide the endurance and stature needed for long-term effectiveness.

It was understandable then that she believed the best way to accomplish this was to put the new program under her direct supervision in the Department of Labor. She could plausibly argue that the new program—with benefits tied to a lifetime of work activity in paid employment—was a natural fit for the responsibilities of the Department.

With the President's ruling on the policy issue, the administrative issue fell into place and the legislative proposal that went to the Congress in January of 1935 envisioned that the public assistance titles of the act would be administered by FERA and the social insurance programs would be administered by the Department of Labor. Perkins thought this settled the matter. But Congress had other ideas.

The House Ways and Means Committee amended the Administration's proposal by combining the two separate types of programs into one agency (keeping the programs themselves distinct) and making that agency independent of both FERA and the Department of Labor. Thus an independent Social Security Board would be responsible for the main titles of the act, with the agency reporting directly to the President. The committee's overt rationale was an apparent unwillingness to place a permanent program in a temporary agency like FERA—and the view that the two types of programs were in fact closely related and thus should be in a single agency. The option of putting them both in the Department of Labor was not adopted because, in the opinion of Arthur Altmeyer, "influential members of both houses of Congress disliked the Department of Labor . . . the personal dislike of the Secretary of Labor was due largely to the fact that she was a woman and an articulate, intelligent woman at that, as well as to the fact that she was not sufficiently amenable to patronage needs."[1]

In her memoir of the New Deal, Perkins reports: "Rather than have any delay, I readily agreed to an independent agency."[2] Well, not too readily. On February 25, she sent an urgent letter to the President alerting him that: "The Ways and Means Committee took further action today . . . that I think you should be aware of. . . . They voted overwhelmingly to set up the Social Insurance Board as a wholly independent agency. . . . You have indicated that the Board should certainly be in the Department of Labor. Otherwise it would be just one more independent bureau, and would be duplicating functions now in the Department. . . . It was said by members that they would change their votes on these points only if you personally urged them to do so and gave good reasons for doing it." (Perkins wrote across the top of the memo, in large cursive script, "I think you will have to speak on telephone to Doughton about this.")[3] The upshot, as Perkins recalled it, was "I talked it over with the President and we agreed that the matter of the place was not a major one on which to make a fight."[4]

This was one of the few battles that Perkins lost in the development of Social Security. Perhaps this was for the best. Even though Frances Perkins served as Secretary of Labor longer than anyone in the nation's history, she was destined to step down eventually, and who knows what future Secretaries of Labor might make of the program. It was better, perhaps, to get the program established with a tradition of administrative independence, rather than as the favored child of even a wise and benevolent political sponsor. In any event, having reached a milestone in 2010, with the 75th anniversary of Social Security in America—the most successful social program in the nation's history— we would have to say that things turned out rather well in the end.

A ROCKY START, BUT AN ENDURING ACHIEVEMENT

Despite Congress giving the new Social Security Board a significant boost by making it an independent agency, this did not settle everything. The question of funding remained. Although the authorizing legislation was signed into law on August 14, 1935, the appropriations for the new agency were contained in a separate bill (the Third Deficiency Appropriation bill). Of the $90 million in the Deficiency bill, $76 million was for the new Social Security Act programs. But the bill got hung up in the Senate when southern and western senators added riders to the legislation raising the subsidies on cotton and wheat. This caused a rift with the House of Representatives, which refused to accept the increased subsidies. The Senate requested a conference with the House to reconcile the two versions of the bill, but the House refused to conference (reportedly the first such refusal in the history of Congress). A deadlock developed, which continued for days. Tempers flared in the Senate—fisticuffs were threatened and angry senators had to be physically restrained by colleagues. When warned that a deadlock would imperil the new Social Security program, House Appropriations

Committee Chairman James Buchanan (D-TX) replied: "We got along for 143 years without a Social Security Board."[5]

Finally, on August 26, the last day of the legislative session, a compromise deal was struck and the Deficiency bill appeared to be saved. At which point, the irascible populist senator from Louisiana, Huey Long, rose to his feet and commenced a one-man filibuster on the bill. Although he was nominally a Democrat, Long was notorious for alienating the leadership of both parties. He once told an audience, "The only difference that I found between the Republican leadership and the Democratic leadership was that one of them was skinning from the ankle up and the other from the ear down, when I got to Congress."[6] Long had no particular objection to the funding for the Social Security Board, but he refused to compromise on the cotton subsidy, so he blocked action on the bill until Congress had to adjourn.

This caused obvious problems for the start-up of Social Security. As an interim strategy, the agency was funded by money borrowed from FERA and with supplies and equipment inherited from the liquidation of the National Recovery Administration (NRA). An irony of the situation was that the FERA monies could be used to pay the staff of the new Social Security Board, but not the three board members themselves. When Altmeyer went to see Secretary Perkins to explain his funding problems, she arose from her red leather office chair, wheeled it around her desk, and pushed it over to Altmeyer, telling him "Here is your first piece of office furniture to get the Board started." (Altmeyer used that chair for the rest of his career.)

Beyond her office chair, Perkins gave much more in this early formative period. Foremost among her contributions was her Assistant Secretary of Labor, Altmeyer. Perkins arranged to have him appointed as one of the three board members, and later, he became the chairman. Putting Altmeyer on the board meant that one of her closest aides would be at the center of the new institution. She later said, "We gave them the best of everything, including Arthur Altmeyer, who was the Assistant

Secretary of Labor and my real right hand, and without whom I felt very lost."[7]

The Department of Labor was really the "parent" of the new Social Security Board, helping it get started in its life. As Perkins put it: ". . . one of the reasons I feel so deeply involved with the Social Security Administration is that even though it was not in the Department of Labor when it was first established, the Department of Labor had to carry it the way you carry a dependent child. It didn't have any money. That was so unfortunate. And we didn't have very much either. What we did, however, was to provide the Social Security Administration with offices in the Department of Labor Building. . . . The whole department did the same kind of thing. We gave them our best statisticians. We gave them the best of everything. . . . It showed that we put our best people in there on loan, and we carried it for the first year and made it look like a going concern. In fact, it became a going concern in an extraordinarily short time."[8]

Secretary Perkins was deeply involved in the initial administrative planning for the start-up of the new program, even worrying over how the agency would keep its massive records on covered workers, a task described at the time as "the largest bookkeeping operation in the world." IBM, a New York-based company, ultimately provided the technological solution, in collaboration with Altmeyer.[9]

THE DEPENDENT CHILD SETS OUT ON ITS OWN

By 1939, the Social Security Board had become its own organization, and Altmeyer had become a formidable figure in his own right. Altmeyer took over as chairman of the board in early 1937, and would go on to serve as head of the Social Security agency until the Eisenhower Administration came into office in 1953. Among the many key New Deal figures, Altmeyer was one of the few whose tenure in government survived the death of President Roosevelt in 1945. Many of the other

New Deal figures who initially stayed on with President Truman were gone by the time of Truman's election in 1948 After the legislative creation of the Social Security program, and its initial administrative launching, it was Altmeyer who, more than any other single person, shaped the nascent program, and especially the organization that would be responsible for administering it.

By the time the crucial 1939 amendments to the Social Security Act were being considered in Congress, Altmeyer had become the acknowledged expert on all aspects of the program—both the grand policies and the deep details. Altmeyer alone was the Administration's witness at the hearings. Having launched the program, Perkins had successfully ensured its continuation by handing it over to her most talented protégé. It didn't come together smoothly at first. Altmeyer had been a state official in Wisconsin's pioneering workmen's compensation program when he started coming to Washington to represent Wisconsin's labor-related interests, in which capacity he came to the attention of Secretary Perkins. Although Altmeyer was not seeking a federal job, he did have hopes, and even expectations, that a federal job might be in the offing.

On several occasions in early 1933, Frances Perkins had asked him to come down to Washington to help with her reorganization of the department, and in particular, to help her straighten out the department's relations with the various state labor departments around the country. There had been hints that a job offer might be forthcoming. Secretary Perkins had let it be known that she was highly impressed with Altmeyer. Despite all the promising signs, however, the expected job offer had not come. By late May of 1934, Altmeyer was losing hope, and he made plans to return to Madison. The morning before his departure, he stopped by Perkins's office to say his good-byes, but she was out so he did not have an opportunity to tell her he was leaving.

He exited the office and strolled over to the Willard Hotel, smoking a cigarette, thinking it was his last day in Washington. A cab stopped at a red light directly in front of him. From the open passenger window someone was shouting something at Altmeyer. It was a tall, dark-haired woman named Mary "Molly" Dewson, an Altmeyer friend, the Democratic Party official in charge of women's issues, and a confidant of both Eleanor Roosevelt and Frances Perkins. "Art," she shouted out. "Wait a couple of days longer." With that, the light turned green and the cab lurched forward, disappearing into the bustle of Washington traffic. A little startled by the surprise message, Altmeyer nevertheless knew that Molly Dewson was a serious person and even a casual communiqué from her was not to be taken lightly, but he was discouraged and decided not to change his plans.

Early the next morning, Frances Perkins was awakened by the persistent ringing of her telephone. "Frances," the voice said. "It's Molly." "Sorry to wake you so early. I wouldn't do it if it wasn't important. I wouldn't even be up myself this early if it weren't important. Don't go anywhere, I'm coming right over to see you."

When Dewson arrived, she didn't waste any time with preliminary chitchat. "Arthur Altmeyer is leaving town in the morning to return to Wisconsin. He's a good man and we need him here in Washington. You've got to give him a job, and quick." Frances Perkins readily agreed with Dewson's assessment of Altmeyer and was receptive to the idea of a job offer. She just hadn't realized the urgency.

In the 1930s, air travel was rare and costly. Altmeyer made his frequent trips to and from Washington by train, in the days before streamlined diesel locomotives plied this route. The trip was a little over 893 miles and took more than 19 hours. Even though Mary Dewson and Frances Perkins were, unbeknownst to him, in conversation about offering him a job, Altmeyer boarded the afternoon train at Union Station, as scheduled, and left for Madison. When he arrived at the station in Madison the next morning he found an urgent telegram from Frances Perkins waiting for him. She wanted him to return immediately. So even though he had just completed a fairly arduous journey, he turned around and did it again—in reverse. When he got back to Washington and went to see Secretary Perkins, she offered him a permanent federal job on the spot, as Assistant Secretary of Labor, and later, a seat on the Social Security Board.

A TRADITION OF INDEPENDENCE

Frances Perkins and President Roosevelt gave substance to the idea that the Social Security program ought to be above partisan politics by recommending John Winant—a nationally prominent Republican—as the first chairman of the board, and by appointing him to the position. Congress, by creating the board as an independent agency, seemed to have a similar objective in mind. They wanted to institutionalize a strong and resilient program. The first challenge came in the 1936 presidential campaign when the Republican candidate, Alf Landon, decided to attack the Social Security system and pledged to abolish it if elected. Winant—who was positioned to be the Republican nominee for Vice President in 1940—resigned from the board and actively campaigned against Landon—ending Winant's own political career. This act of political courage by Winant was a crucial early test of the ability of the program to maintain a measure of independence from political pressures.

The next test was an unexpected one. A law dating from the nineteenth century prohibited federal employees from assisting persons making claims against the government—the idea being to prevent fraudulent collusion between a corrupt government official and someone trying to make an unjustified claim on federal monies. The General Accounting Office (GAO) issued a ruling stating that the board could not assist claimants for Social Security benefits in pursuing their claims. Altmeyer forcefully resisted the GAO, arguing that Social Security benefits were earned rights and that the government had *a positive obligation* to assist applicants in attaining their rightful benefits.

Had the GAO prevailed, the administration of the program would have been radically different, and probably many fewer people would have qualified for benefits. Altmeyer's assertion of the program's unique status resulted in a concession, stated in the best bureaucratic fashion. The GAO conceded that the government "was not required to object."

In 1939, the program's independence was again put to a test when the board lost its status as an independent agency and was made part of the new Federal Security Agency (FSA). Even though Altmeyer thereby became the subordinate of the FSA administrator, his stature was such that the agency continued to operate with an astonishing degree of independence—proving again that Perkins' choice of Altmeyer was shrewd indeed. By 1994, Congress had become concerned once again that the agency was subject to too much political pressure and so it enacted (by a unanimous vote in both houses of Congress) a law returning the organization to its original status as an independent agency.

THE GROWTH OF THE PROGRAM

The Social Security program that Frances Perkins bequeathed to the nation in 1934–1935 was profound in conception but modest in scope. It covered only about half the workers in the economy. It initially paid only retirement benefits, and only to the individual worker himself/ herself. It would not collect its first payroll taxes until 1937, and would not start paying monthly benefits until 1940. By the end of that first year, there were only about 222,000 people receiving benefits; and the average benefit amount was less than $20 a month.

By the time Frances Perkins came to Social Security's headquarters in October of 1962 to deliver her valedictory speech on the founding of the program, the landscape had changed considerably. Whole new types of benefits had been added to the program: dependents' and survivors' benefits in 1939; disability benefits in 1956; early retirement options in 1956 and 1961. There were more than 18 million beneficiaries by that time, and the average monthly benefit had nearly quadrupled. The program had gone from paying out $4 million a month to paying out about $1.2 billion each month.

The last two major pieces of the modern program had yet to be put in place. Medicare would arrive in 1965, and annual Cost of Living Adjustments (COLAs) would be enacted in 1972. She would not live to see either, but both were logical outgrowths of the program she helped design and implement.

Today, the Social Security program is colossal in scope, but not all that different in basic conception from the one created by Frances Perkins. Today, there are over 54 million Social Security beneficiaries, and the program pays out more than $700 billion in annual benefits. For much of the last twenty years, the Social Security program has been the largest single function in the federal government's budget. Indeed, the amount of money flowing through the system each year is greater than the entire economies of all but the fifteen or so richest nations in the world.

The Social Security program is the largest, and arguably the most successful, social program ever undertaken by the federal government. It plays a massive and crucial role in the life of the nation. If Frances Perkins were still with us today, she, no doubt, would look upon her creation with a large measure of satisfaction. At Mount Holyoke College her class motto was "Be Ye Steadfast," and she pronounced herself an adherent to the philosophy of Holyoke's founder, Mary Lyon, who admonished her students that they "should live for God and do something." When it comes to Social Security, Frances Perkins certainly did something.

MY FATHER passed away when my sister and I were age 5 and 7, respectively. I can't remember what the months were like proceeding or following his death, but I do have a few vivid memories of him.

He was a plastic surgeon, and we lived considerably well in a small town in New Jersey. My mother had been a retired special education teacher since my sister was born, and she last worked in a school district in Philadelphia, PA. When my father passed, somehow my mother was able to hold it together and figure out how to organize the family and keep going. I can't imagine the strength she had to have used to keep our family from losing our home, moving, and changing our lives. I asked her only a few years ago what she would have done if we had not had the support from survivors benefits, and she replied that we probably would have moved back to Philly, and my whole life could have been drastically changed.

Instead, Social Security helped provide meaningful support for my family until I graduated from high school. Both my sister and I were able to go to college, and now we both have great jobs.

I never thought I would end up working for Social Security, but now that I am here, I am so grateful for the program's existence.

In the event that nothing drastically changes in future years, I may be one of only a few that has received some form of benefit or compensation from Social Security for almost my entire life.

— ERICK CHALFIN —
REDDING, CALIFORNIA

A Fierce Determination to Improve: Social Security and IBM

PAUL C. LASEWICZ

Paul C. Lasewicz is the corporate archivist for the
IBM Corporation. A frequent presenter at professional
conferences, he has published on a variety of
topics relating to corporate archives, ranging from
international records management to knowledge
management to privacy to the role heritage plays
in corporate brands. There are more than a dozen
members of his family currently collecting Social
Security benefits.

*O*n August 14, 1935, with a stroke of a pen, President Franklin Roosevelt set in motion a chain of events that in two years would change the lives of generations of Americans. It would also create what the nation's press would trumpet as the largest bookkeeping job in the world—creating and updating on a lifetime basis individual wage records for the nation's estimated 26 million workers.

The pioneering technology partnership between the Social Security Administration and IBM was crucial to the success of the Social Security Act, a piece of New Deal legislation that has affected hundreds of millions of American workers and their families since its inception in 1937. At a Social Security Administration employee event marking the 25th anniversary of the Act becoming law, Secretary of Labor Frances Perkins recalled how critical to the successful implementation of the Act a technology solution was, and how worrisome a problem it was. "IBM hadn't invented the machines you all operate so easily," she said. "And I want you to realize that it took some courage to launch the program without the IBM machines. I would like to add that under any circumstances I was always a bit nervous about it, and I remember the day that Arthur Altmeyer, who was then First Assistant Secretary of Labor, walked into my office and said, 'You know, I think we found it.' Because he had been talking about, you know, handwritten pieces of records and how they were to be organized and stacked up. 'I think we found it. These new IBM machines, I believe they can do it.' And so out of that really inventive group that worked in the IBM research group, we found a way by which this could be done."[1]

The technology solution that was collaboratively developed by the Social Security Administration and IBM traced its roots to 1920, when the U. S. Department of Agriculture and IBM developed a punched card accounting system for agricultural research. Elwood Way, a Department of Agriculture employee with two years of service, was the first to suggest using punched cards to coordinate data. This suggestion, Way later recalled, was based on once seeing IBM machines in action at the Pillsbury Milling Company in Minneapolis. He had no real experience with punched card equipment per se, but since it was his idea, he got "stuck with the job." Way quickly became a punched card systems expert, and during his decade with what became known as the Machine Tabulating and Computing Section of the Bureau of Markets, he oversaw more than 100 tabulating projects—some one-time studies, other larger recurring jobs.[2]

The growth and development of punched card system expertise in the government accelerated during the early days of Roosevelt's New Deal, which saw the creation of a series of accounting system projects, each larger and far more reaching than its predecessor.

In June of 1933, Way took on the task of creating an accounting system for the Agricultural Adjustment Administration's (AAA) Cotton Control Contract, which would manage contracts with more than 1.6 million cotton farmers. During this effort he met Henry P. Seidemann, who was "without question at the time the top expert in the field of [fiscal] recordkeeping in the United States." Seidemann was impressed with Way's combination of knowledge of accounting and punched card systems, and the two formed a working relationship that would later pay dividends for the Social Security Administration.[3] The AAA project was the largest accounting system yet tackled by the government, and its successful and speedy implementation developed expertise within both the government and IBM that would later prove critical during the roll out of the Social Security system.[4] But at the time, the quick installation of the punched card system had more immediate benefits, according to Dr. Rexford Tugwell, Under Secretary for the Department of Agriculture. "It's a wonder. We got out these checks with it, and if we hadn't gotten them out on time we would have had a revolution. Farmers were calling for those checks and there was no way in the world to get them out except by such devices as this company produces and furnishes to the country."[5]

In October of 1934, Way was recruited by Murray Latimer to work on the Railroad Retirement Board (RRB). Latimer was the Chairman of the RRB, and he was familiar with Way's work on the AAA project. The RRB intended to create an accounting system to track the retirement funds for some 3.5 million employees whose deductions would be taken from their wages and posted to an interest-bearing account.

Way started from scratch with no staff and no equipment, but enjoyed "considerable latitude in the development of plans." He consulted a few individuals from a growing circle of government punched card system experts: Tom McDonald from the Department of Agriculture days, as well as Joseph Fay and others from Way's other punched card projects. He recruited two men who had previously participated in a study of the railroad retirement issue in New York: Robert H. LaMotte, who had expertise with IBM equipment; and Francis E. Fleener, previously associated with the Interstate Commerce Commission. The general concept that Way's team worked out for the Railroad Retirement Board called for IBM punched card machines to be the workhorses of the operation. But in May of 1935, before the board could order the equipment, the Railroad Retirement Board was declared unconstitutional, and the plan was scrapped.[6] The development work, however, was not wasted, in that many of the process concepts that were developed for the RRB would later influence the system design for the Social Security program.[7]

In the meantime, Way, LaMotte, and Fleener had little time to mourn the passing of their project. Within a month, they all moved to the Treasury Department, where they were immediately charged with designing a record keeping process for the Emergency Relief Act of 1935. "They didn't have time to give me a title," Way recalled. "We secured quarters and got equipment fast . . . and were in business within a few weeks."[8]

Soon after Roosevelt signed the Social Security Act on August 14, 1935, Way, several former colleagues from the AAA, and an IBM representative were invited to a working lunch at the Brookings Institute by Seidemann, who showed them copies of the Act. Seidemann pointed out that the Act itself gave no hint as to how the program was going to be accomplished. "Congress had not prescribed how the records would be kept," a long-time Social Security employee later recounted. "There is nothing in there that says anything with respect to the types of records we will maintain."[9] Seidemann asked the group to think about possible plans of attack.[10]

In September, Way returned for another lunch at the Brookings Institute and was introduced by Seidemann to Governor John G. Winant. Winant, a lanky man with bushy eyebrows who cut a figure reminiscent of Abraham Lincoln, was a member of Brookings's Board of Directors. Eventually Winant would become Ambassador to Great Britain, but he was in short order to be appointed the first Chairman of the Social Security Board. Intrigued by Way's work at the Treasury Department, Winant was, according to Way, "quite pleased" with what he learned about punched card systems. Winant closed the meeting by telling Way "I hope to see you again. I hope I see you constantly."

Not long after, Way received a call from Arthur Altmeyer, the Second Assistant to the Secretary of the Department of Labor (and future executive director of the Social Security Administration), asking him to devise a budget for the Social Security registration job. In November of 1935, Way was appointed a Special Assistant to the Secretary of Labor Frances Perkins, without ever having even met her.[11] Way reported to Seidemann but once again worked independently helping to develop the budget and identifying staffing and equipment requirements. Eventually he received the title Chief of the Records Division.

Meanwhile, funding for the Social Security program was held up when Louisiana's legendary Senator Huey Long engaged in a session-ending filibuster, which resulted in the Senate adjourning for winter recess without passing several appropriations measures. The fledgling Social Security Board, with its leaders appointed but lacking a budget of its own, was forced to borrow space, furniture, and clerical help from Frances Perkins's Department of Labor. Perkins's help was an act of faith. "She didn't know quite—and neither did anybody else, of course, exactly all that was involved, how long it would take to set up the machinery," recalled Latimer, who also later joined Social Security.[12] The board was slated to go into operation on January 1, 1937, but Long's filibuster caused a delay that the organization, already under tight time constraints and facing a daunting task of almost unimaginable scope, could ill afford.

The task at hand was nothing less than developing and maintaining a complete lifetime record of all wages paid to America's workforce. As of January of 1942, every qualified individual more than 65 years of age would receive a monthly benefit. This benefit would be based on a calculation derived from the total wages the individual had earned after December 31, 1936. For those who died before age 65, a lump-sum payment based on a percentage of total earnings after December 31, 1936, would be paid to their heirs. Starting on January 1, 1937, the Social Security Board was required by law to create files for an estimated 26 million American workers, and to tabulate on a quarterly basis a percentage of the earnings of these workers to their accounts.[13]

As of January 1, 1936, there was little hope that any of this could be done in time. The process for identifying workers and collecting this highly personal information was unclear. The same was true for the processes of tabulating, maintaining the funds, and making payments to eligible workers. The prospect of finding enough trained record keeping personnel was in doubt. The constitutionality of the Social Security Act itself was still very much in question, and the political climate for the program was by no means one of universal support. Since any one of these obstacles was enough to undermine the program, it was no wonder that some of the social insurance experts the board consulted held little hope for success.[14]

Nonetheless, the Social Security Administration finally received its funding in February when Congress reconvened for its winter session. By late April the board's Committee on Old-Age Benefits Records and Methods had drafted a document for approximately 190 manufacturers of business equipment. The document detailed the problems the board was facing, and noted the board's interest in creating a collaborative solution for record keeping and management. In order for a proposal to be considered, it would have to completely outline an entire accounting system, listing required equipment, proposed methods and procedures, estimated manpower and space needs, and costs.[15]

Curiously, despite the press of time, the board didn't act on the document immediately. Way, for one, recalled later that he didn't believe getting a plan in place was a pressing matter. That lack of urgency could have been in part a reflection of Winant's management style, which emphasized face-to-face communication, and a meticulous, personal attention to details. He was, much to the chagrin of his executive assistant, a man who personally signed every letter that went out under his name, no matter how insignificant.[16] It wasn't until June 15 when the board finally swung into action, sending letters inviting proposals to about 100 business equipment companies.

During the course of the summer, the board began receiving proposals. On several occasions they asked a responding company for a supplementary proposal to further clarify what they felt were gaps in the original submission. By August the board had identified nine proposals that it thought were complete enough to go forward with, and on August 19, it formally created an Equipment Committee (officially, the Committee on Old-Age Benefits Equipment, Records, and Methods) to consider the proposals in more detail. The members of the committee—most notably Seideman, Way, Fay, Beach, Fleener—were representative of a key group of early Social Security hires who were "machine people"—individuals who had previous experience with punched card equipment.[17] "I say that that whole group was really a bonanza for the Social Security organization," Way later reflected. "They had worked on a similar problem—worked together, as someone might say, spoke the same language. They provided a nucleus for the whole accounting operations, there's no doubt about that."[18] The committee quickly scheduled hearings with each of the companies to discuss the proposals.

IBM was the first company to meet with the committee, and the IBM team was more than ready to go. The company's lead salesman on the account, H.J. McDonald, recounted years later that IBM had been preparing for the proposal for two years, even before the Act was officially passed in August of 1935. IBM's primary internal publication, Business Machines, had been hammering away at the business opportunity Social Security represented throughout all of 1936—speeches by Winant and Seidemann were reprinted in full during the year.

Significantly, IBM President Thomas J. Watson, Sr., was personally involved in the proposal. "Mr. Watson wanted the S.S. account more than anything else in the world, and by the way . . . he was the one who helped us tremendously on that," McDonald recalled. "He told me himself, 'McDonald, I want that job regardless. . . .We want that business and will give you anything you need to get it.'"[19] As McDonald worked on the proposal with C. Ross Green and other colleagues from IBM's Methods Research Department at World Headquarters in New

York City, the team was under the personal direction of Watson, Sr. The legendary businessman, known as America's "$1,000 a Day Man" because of his well-publicized annual salary, required a daily report of the progress being made. He also attended many of the team's discussion sessions, giving advice and counsel as to methods and equipment.[20]

At 11:00 A.M. on Wednesday, August 19, IBM Washington office representatives R. Brinkley Smithers, McDonald, Green, and another member of the company's Methods Research staff, met with the Equipment Committee in the Social Security Boardroom. Smithers, the son of one of IBM's largest shareholders, was a rising star at IBM. Having worked for his father's firm on Wall Street for much of his twenties, Smithers struck out on his own and joined IBM in October of 1931, as a student clerk in the company's New York office. He performed impressively, was sent to IBM's sales school in June of 1932, and was promoted to senior salesman in May of the following year. In 1934, his first full year as a salesman, he achieved a remarkable 187 percent of quota, earning membership in IBM's prestigious Hundred Percent Club. More significantly, Smithers seemed to have a knack for recruiting completely new clients—a full 69 percent of his sales in 1934 were to new customers, including two clients who were in industries that had never used IBM tabulating equipment before. Because of these entrepreneurial instincts, Smithers was promoted to assistant manager in IBM's Washington, D.C. office in January of 1935.

Smithers's presence at this first meeting was a strategic move on IBM's part. A veteran of the New York metropolitan social scene, Smithers had excellent interpersonal skills and was an accomplished relationship builder. The fact that Smithers did not participate in follow-up meetings was also no accident—he was much more comfortable at breaking the ice and building personal relationships than immersing himself in the intricacies of punched card operations.

For its part, the Social Security Board brought its heavy hitters to the table—Altmeyer, Latimer, Seidemann, Way, Fay, Fleener, John

Deviney, and Charles Beach—the top executives and the leading machine people. After a brief introductory statement by McDonald, the IBM team provided a walk through on how the estimates were prepared. The committee, led by Altmeyer, began questioning the IBM team in more detail about the proposal. According to the official committee minutes of the meeting, the "questions were satisfactorily explained to the Committee by the members of the I.B.M. Company." After a two-hour discussion, the meeting adjourned, and a follow-up meeting was scheduled for the following Tuesday, August 25.[21]

The prospective partners resumed the discussion that Tuesday at 2:30 P.M. in the Social Security Boardroom. On hand for IBM were McDonald and three colleagues providing technical expertise. Among those representing the committee were Seidemann, Fleener, Way, Fay, Deviney, and Beach. During this meeting, the proposal was discussed in great detail, with Fleener acting as the lead questioner for the committee. The committee's primary focus during this discussion was to reduce the rental costs of the IBM equipment by reducing the number of machines required. Since labor was the cheapest component of the tabulating equation, the committee counter-proposed that IBM revise their proposal to include less machines on the presumption that multiple shifts would be employed. The IBM representatives assented, and agreed to resubmit their proposal by the following Wednesday. The committee minutes of the meeting, likely taken by Beach, noted that "On the whole, this was the most satisfactory meeting. There was general agreement among all of us that the plan submitted by the IBM, with slight modifications, would answer all requirements of the Records Division from accounting, statistical, and actuarial standpoints."[22]

Still, there were key aspects of the proposal still left undone. In particular, the IBMers had included in their proposal designs for two yet-to-be designed machines, a collator and a posting machine. Both of these machines were absolutely critical to the successful execution of the Social Security project, and that they did not in fact yet exist was a source of some consternation at the highest levels of government.[23]

Over the next couple of weeks, the committee met with eight additional vendors, assessed their proposals, and settled on three finalists. Two of the vendor proposals offered similar solutions, based on the use of bookkeeping methods, whereas the IBM solution proposed the use of electric accounting machines and punched cards. Finding themselves struggling with differentiating between the three proposals, the committee decided to focus first on comparing the relative merits of the two methods.

Viewed from that perspective, it became a clear-cut decision. "It was," one Social Security executive later recalled, "easily determined that the punched card system was the cheapest, would get all the required information, and give a finalized posted individual record. And they [IBM] were awarded the contract."[24]

The written record leaves much unsaid about other considerations that may have factored into the decision to award IBM the Social Security contract. Certainly the aggressive efforts of the IBM team, led by the personal attention of Watson Sr., indicated to the committee that the project would get the full attention and weight of the IBM Corporation. Certainly IBM's successful track record in dealing with the increasing scale of prior federal accounting projects influenced the committee as well.

Likewise, the fact that so many of the Social Security Committee members had—through those earlier federal punched card projects— accrued significant past experience with IBM processes, technology, personnel, and service levels undoubtedly played a factor in raising their individual comfort levels with the proposal. That level of familiarity extended to members of the Social Security Board itself. Vincent M. Miles, one of the three original board members, in a speech in June of 1936, before a convention of heating ventilation and air conditioning contractors, demonstrated his hands-on familiarity with IBM when he spoke of the positive benefits of air conditioning at a corporate manufacturing facility in upstate New York. Although he didn't name the firm, that facility was in fact IBM's Endicott plant.[15] Personal relationships were an important part of the proposal assessments, because it was clear from the start that in order for the project to succeed, it would require a highly collaborative partnership between the board and the winning contractor.

One could ask whether it is possible that these unwritten factors meant that IBM was predetermined to win the Social Security contract. Clearly, the committee worked very closely with several of the other vendors to make their initial proposals more complete and competitive. And there was no guarantee that the IBM proposal itself would be successful, because it relied on significant, yet to be developed technologies. So it is difficult to determine in retrospect whether or not the committee was predisposed to IBM during the proposal process. But it is not a stretch to conclude that the contract was IBM's to lose.

The fact that the IBM proposal was the first to be vetted is particularly revealing in this regard. It indicates that the committee expected that IBM would, based on its familiarity with prior federal accounting projects, provide a detailed and informed outline of what would be required to tackle a project of this scale. IBM's initial outline would not only set the bar for other proposals to be compared against, it would also serve to educate the less knowledgeable committee members as to the issues and processes involved. The fact that the record indicates the committee was noticeably more informed in regard to, and critical of, the initial proposals of the other companies indicates that the IBM proposal did indeed fulfill these expectations.

Ultimately, the cumulative weight of all these factors, both written and unwritten, led the committee to select the IBM proposal for recommendation to the board. Committee chairman Seidemann submitted under his signature the *Committee on Old-Age Benefits Records and Methods Summary Report and Recommendations to the Members of the Social Security Board* on September 16, 1936. The report recommended that the IBM proposal be accepted.

Perhaps reflecting a desire to streamline the bureaucratic process, it also asked that the committee be authorized to negotiate directly with IBM ". . . any further refinements or improvements that it may be advisable to make . . ." to the proposed procedures or equipment. This request may have been inserted in part as a response to the perceived foot-dragging on the part of the Social Security Board during the proposal review process.[26]

But this request may have also reflected the rushed nature of the negotiations, for as Way later recounted, "We didn't negotiate very deeply about the machines. We needed them quickly and they were willing to put them in."[27] In this scenario, where time was of the essence, the committee was focused on defining the broad sweeps of the process, and pragmatically recognizing that there were many details that would have to be worked out after the contract was signed. Acting with more urgency than it had in April, the Social Security Board approved the IBM proposal on September 16, the very same day it received Seidemann's recommendation.

The initial installation of the Social Security equipment was supposed to be located in Washington D.C., the traditional seat of the federal government. But this proved not to be. "I remember," Way recalled later, "going out with John Deviney and Merton Emerson in Washington, looking at big apartment buildings, vacant factory buildings. . . .[and] We could find nothing available that had sufficient floor space."[28] Other structural requirements further narrowed the pool of qualified properties. The new facility had to be fire resistant to protect the tens of millions of paper records it would house. It had to have sufficient floor strength to support the weight of the IBM machines and the thousands of file cabinets. It also had to be available on a temporary lease basis, because the near term plan was to build and relocate to a Washington office building.[29]

After failure to find a structure that met these requirements in

Washington, the Social Security administrators then looked about 40 miles north to Baltimore, Maryland. There they located a former Coca-Cola bottling plant on Baltimore's bustling Pier 5 waterfront, known locally as the Candler Building.

"I'll never forget as long as I live," Tom McDonald later wrote, "the day I first walked in there. The whole place was dilapidated, unpainted, and forbidding."[30] It was coat-wearing cold in the winter, unbearably hot in the summer, and had fleas populating the sound-deadening sand underneath the hardwood floors.[31] It was also prone to invasion by the smells produced by its busy waterfront neighbors—dead fish from the wharves, spicy aromas from the McCormick Company, and foul chemical odors from a local drug manufacturer. In addition to these neighbors, there was also a noisy outdoor market, and a cheap saloon on every corner.[32] It lacked a cafeteria, and it had segregated restrooms that were intended for a much smaller workforce.

It wasn't exactly the white collar environment the board had envisioned for its new, highly educated workforce. The board's executive director, Frank Bane, later recalled his disappointment with the Candler. "As we walked through that old warehouse-type structure," he wrote, "my heart sank. There seemed to be no other choice, however."[33] So the rental lease was signed, and on November 9, 1936, the first contingent of Social Security employees from Washington moved in under the leadership of Baltimore operations chief Joseph Fay. By late December, nearly a third of the 2,200 employees on board were working under the guidance of a large staff of IBM trainers, using dummy cards to simulate the exact processes they would soon be using for real.[34]

While these employees were rapidly filling the three leased floors of the Candler, IBM was installing its equipment. By the first week of December, the company had moved in 284 Alphabetical Punches, 67 Horizontal Sorters, 37 Alphabetic Tabulators, and a host of smaller peripheral machines. But reflecting the collaborative nature of the project, IBM personnel were not just installing machines; they were partnering with Social Security staff to create the machine techniques and records processes that would form the very heart of the project.

Many of these processes were based on existing procedures and techniques that had been developed for prior federal punched card installations. According to Way, "There were frequent instances where procedures which had been successful there were adopted bodily for use in Social Security. Working in block units, accounting for mechanic machine time, wall charts depicting flow of work [sic]. These things were all concepts with which this group had some experience. There were also frequent instances in which something needed in [that] former work had been developed in the interim by IBM."[35]

In addition to these process modifications, there were technical tweaks being made as well. "A great many improvements were made in the functioning of the machines during the time in which this procedure was being planned," Way later recalled. "They were of varied nature, some being changes in the functioning of electrical circuits, while others required structural changes in mechanical features of a machine. The IBM staff was in continuous contact with the staff engaged in developing procedures and presumably developed significant changes without specific requests by the Social Security staff."[36] These technical improvements were considered relatively simple at the time, but cumulatively they had a significant impact on the evolving Social Security system.

While the operation was ramping up in December, massive amounts of employee records were already arriving—400,000 per day on average were being delivered to the Candler, with a one-day high of 1.3 million— creating an intimidating backlog for the fledgling operation. But by early April of 1937, the increasingly efficient Social Security team had caught up with the mountains of paper. In a milestone ceremony that was broadcast live over the NBC Blue radio network, the 26 millionth account card was punched, just 94 and a half days after the first account had been created. The clatter of the IBM machines could be heard in the background as Frances Perkins, Altmeyer, and Fay were interviewed to mark the occasion.[37]

Despite the celebration, there was still much work left to be done to make Social Security a reality, for the creation of the accounts was just the first phase of the operation. What remained was establishing the ongoing process for tracking and integrating individual weekly payroll information in each account. For this task, the promised but as yet undelivered IBM collators would be the linchpin of the integration process. "IBM, in getting the contract on the basis of its proposal, had agreed to furnish us with two new and special pieces of equipment that had never been used before in punch card work," a Social Security employee recalled some years later. "They guaranteed, come June of 1937, that they would have on our floors machines that would actually take two files of cards matched and merged, rejects and unmatches. They did it."[38] The first IBM collating machines arrived from Endicott on June 30, 1937. Once the collators were in place, the organization had everything it needed to begin merging employee payroll data into existing individual accounts. In less than two years after it became the law of the land, the vague, ambiguous language of the 1935 Social Security Act had been deciphered, interpreted, designed, and fully operationalized.

This partnership between the Social Security Board and IBM to construct a system to mechanically process tens of millions of individual worker accounts—the largest accounting project ever seen—was a modern marvel, even to those closely associated with the Administration. In 1937, Mary W. Dewson, a Social Security Board member, wrote to IBM President Thomas J. Watson, "Well, since I have been over to Baltimore and seen the I.B.M. machines in our office there, I have been more and more impressed. These robot machines have made the tremendous physical task of the Social Security Board possible. This is not a public testimonial, but just an expression of amazement from one who had not kept up with the progress of automatic recording."[39]

For its part, IBM derived immense benefits from the Social Security partnership. It was the company's largest accounting contract to date, and provided much needed cash flow during the difficult days of the Depression. Significantly, the new business went beyond the actual dollars spent by the government to include business generated by the new record keeping requirements that the Social Security Act made incumbent upon employers. In late 1936, the company estimated that the Act's requirements had created an additional 20,000 prospects for equipment that would help employers track and create records to send to Social Security.[40] Six months later, the company's primary publication, *Business Machines*, noted with no small satisfaction that the company's Service Bureau was managing to keep pace with the increased business generated by the employer requirements mandated by the Act.[41] By the end of 1937, IBM's revenues were $31 million, an increase of 48 percent over 1935's figures, and by 1939, revenues were 81 percent higher than 1935.

Equally important to IBM was the experience the company garnered during the project and the credibility with the government and the industry that experience created. IBM's Louis "Red" LaMotte, who headed up IBM's entire federal account during the war years, stated that the Social Security partnership "demonstrated IBM's originality in development and engineering and the company's willingness to constantly undertake something new."[42]

Sixty years after the original installation, a long-time Social Security employee could still recall that IBM was happy to use the installation as a place to test new ideas. "I can't over-stress the fact that Social Security was," he said, "if not the only, certainly the best organization for IBM to work with to do this kind of innovative development." For many years the company utilized the Social Security installation in Baltimore for business purposes, bringing corporate visitors to the Candler to see what was widely considered as a "model" site for IBM technologies.[43]

Both IBM and Social Security derived benefits from their pioneering partnership, and the trust it engendered between IBM and the broader federal government served as the foundation for IBM's central role in the dramatic expansion of governmental data processing over the next 30 years. As the government increasingly turned to technology to help overcome the logistical and computational challenges posed by the Second World War, the Cold War, the space program, and Medicare, IBM—by dint of its Social Security expertise—was well positioned to become a primary partner in the design and implementation of data processing solutions for these national issues. For that reason, IBM's 1936 contract with the Social Security Administration remains to this day a significant and celebrated moment in the company's history.

SOCIAL SECURITY preserved my family. My father was a carpenter. He loved building things. He was almost 40 when he married and started building a family.

My mother was a housewife. As part of the rent for our apartment in Buchanan, New York, my father helped maintain the building.

On April 22, 1972, my father had a sudden, massive heart attack while tending the furnace in our building. I was eight years old; I had three older brothers and two younger ones. As I watched the paramedics wheel my father's body out to the ambulance, I worried about who was going to support my family.

After my father's funeral, my mother applied for Social Security survivors benefits, which we began receiving within weeks.

Each month, after our seven Social Security checks had cleared, my mother, brothers, and I headed for the supermarket, where we filled three grocery carts full of nonperishable food—six growing boys ate a lot.

Although she started working after my father died, without the Social Security survivors benefits that we received, my mother could not have afforded to raise my brothers and me together. We would have been split up, and most of us would have been sent to live with relatives, or would have been placed in foster care.

Which is not to say that we lived extravagantly. We were frugal, but there were times at the end of the month when we were just about out of food. My mother always worried that she wouldn't be able to afford to keep our family together.

My brothers and I all worked, to contribute to the household. The Social Security benefits, by themselves, just weren't enough, although they later helped me pay for college.

— STEFAN LONCE —
CROTON-ON-HUDSON, NEW YORK

127

Robert Ball's Life Work

JONATHAN BALL

Jonathan Ball is a practicing psychotherapist. His mother, now age 97, and his wife, a retired schoolteacher, are Social Security recipients.

*T*he words "Social Security" may have been spoken more times in my family than in any other family on the planet. My father was the late Robert M. Ball. Social Security was his life's work. It was a life's work that spanned 68 of the 75 years of Social Security's existence. Here are some reflections on how his life with Social Security appeared to a family member. Note that it is becoming possible to learn more about how it appeared to him as parts of his memoir are edited and published. His longtime co-author and colleague, Tom Bethell, has recently published a first chapter—"The Greenspan Commission, What Really Happened" (The Century Foundation Press, 2010).

I must have first heard the words "Social Security" as a newborn living in West Annapolis. Three years into his career, with a first child on the way, my father made the move from field office work to Headquarters, which by then had moved to Baltimore as office space in D.C. had become tight. However, Baltimore was experiencing an apartment shortage. My parents rented a house on a farm in West Annapolis from which he could commute by the one-car local train to work. Before we moved again, I had come to understand that Social Security was the place at the other end of that train line. Later on, I visited his office in the Equitable Building, looked at the punch card operation in the Candler Building, and could see that Social Security was more than a train station. Much later, when I was 13, my parents took me with them to a field in Woodlawn to envision with them what would become the new Social Security complex.

I gained the concept of Social Security as a job that involved helping people. It was a less tangible help than that provided by a police officer or firefighter, but apparently had somewhat the same importance for the health of the community. It was about protecting people from hard times. It was a kind of protection people deserved and that they had earned. I came to see that in this way Social Security was a noble calling, a cause to be pursued, beyond being a job.

Two years ago, Commissioner Astrue and Regional Commissioner Disman put on an event to honor my father in Newark, New Jersey, where he began his career in 1939. Attending that event helped me understand the organizational climate during that early stage in the program and my father's response to it as an entry-level field assistant. It was evident that Social Security was a calling for him from the very start. He believed President Roosevelt's vision that this controversial new program could provide a vital addition to the American way of life. He believed that an effective Social Security program could become a manifestation of government at its best. This perspective continued to inform his approach as he moved on to the analysis division, then the training office, and on through a series of leadership positions. Indeed, for the rest of his life, he felt responsible for the well-being of Social Security as an institution.

By the time I was in high school I understood that this institution was important in the history of our country and that it needed to grow. Seeing my father play a role, usually behind the scenes, in the legislative dramas that continued to shape this part of history was very exciting. At some crucial moments, I was able to be in the audience for Ways and Means Committee hearings and to be in the gallery for Senate deliberations. It was after I was away in college that President Kennedy appointed my father Commissioner of Social Security. From then on, my father was at the center of even more dramatic steps in Social Security's history, including the enactment and implementation of Medicare. A comprehensive account of my father's career with an emphasis on policy making can be found in Ed Berkowitz's biography, *Robert Ball and the Politics of Social Security* (University of Wisconsin Press, 2003).

Family members sometimes teased my father that even though he was one of the leading experts on retirement he never figured out how to retire himself. When he resigned in the second Nixon Administration after being the longest serving Commissioner, he went on to a second Social Security career. His activities included creating The National Academy of Social Insurance to bring together experts who could enhance America's understanding and valuing of social insurance. He tirelessly worked to protect and advance the basic principles of Social Security. More often than not change in politics dictated that he assume the role of defender. He helped defeat major attempts to compromise the program in 1983, 1996, and 2005. Tom Bethell has written a lively account of this last conflict over privatization (See "Roosevelt Redux, Robert M. Ball and the Battle for Social Security," *The American Scholar*, Spring 2005 and Summer 2005). His defending never stopped. My father's final piece of writing, which is the basis for the newly published memoir chapter, was his effort to stave off any potential damage that could arise from the creation of a future commission (such as the current National Commission on Fiscal Responsibility and Reform).

On the 70th anniversary of Social Security, I had the unusual experience of standing in for my father at Hyde Park. He was presented with the Franklin D. Roosevelt Distinguished Public Service Award by the Franklin and Eleanor Roosevelt Institute. I knew he had a number of heroes, but I felt confident in responding to the presentation by saying "No honor could be more gratifying to him or to our family than to have his career and his legacy associated with Franklin Roosevelt. It is the FDR approach to public service and social policy that my father strove to bring to his life's work—the persistent optimism, the mixture of idealism and pragmatism, the dynamic vision of a more just America. It is the FDR kind of impact on our nation's well-being that my father has sought to augment in his own areas of endeavor."

Since my father's death in January of 2008, I have had in my study the impressive bust of FDR he was awarded at Hyde Park. It represents his life's work coming full circle. If my father were here to comment on these reflections for the 75th anniversary, he would probably say that I said too much about him—it is the future of the institution of Social Security that is important, not the actions of one person.

SOCIAL SECURITY virtually saved me from a very real possibility of a life in a dumpster. Gave me a shot at sanity, sobriety, and a . . . life.

Given that life and the stability that Social Security provided, I am now engaged in an encore (professional) career. Got back to productivity. No life on the couch for this guy, but I wouldn't have had it save for the blessings of this terrific program. So THNX—FDR.

P.S. HATED payin' into it—the whole of my life. (Raised very right-wing. Any excuse to avoid any "contribution." So, so glad I was made to save because I surely would not have otherwise.)

— JAMES TAYLOR —
REED POINT, MONTANA

The Impact of Social Security on American Lives

NANCY J. ALTMAN

Nancy Altman, author of *The Battle for Social Security*, has a
thirty-year background in the areas of private pensions and
Social Security. She is currently the chairman of the Board of
Directors of the Pension Rights Center, a nonprofit organization
dedicated to the protection of beneficiary rights. From 1983
to 1989, Altman was on the faculty of Harvard University's
Kennedy School of Government and taught courses on private
pensions and Social Security at the Harvard Law School. In
1982, she was Alan Greenspan's assistant in his position as
chairman of the bipartisan commission that developed the
1983 Social Security amendments. She comes from a long-lived
family. Her mother died at age 95 and Social Security added
to the comfort of her final years. Social Security disability
insurance is the primary personal source of income for Nancy's
brother-in-law, who suffered an incapacitating back injury and
can no longer work.

*S*ocial Security has transformed the United States. Before Social Security, people worked as long as they could hold jobs, but that was an insecure state of affairs. The fast pace of many jobs "wears out its workers with great rapidity," a commentator noted in 1912. "The young, the vigorous, the adaptable, the supple of limb, the alert of mind are in demand," he explained, adding, "Middle age is old age."[1] Once a job was lost, an older worker could seldom find a new one. Indeed, want ads at the time often specified age restrictions.

Once out of work, older people almost never had sufficient savings to last until death. The dilemma of saving for one's own retirement was described in 1934:

> A man's productive, wage-earning period is rarely more than 45 years. Under present conditions he must earn enough in this period to contribute toward the support of aged parents, rear and educate children, maintain his family at a standard of living more or less consistent with American ideals, and save enough in the form of insurance or absolutely safe investment to provide a modest income until death, if he survives his working period. This last item of his budget is the one least urgent, least stressed by advertising propaganda and most easily disregarded among the many financial demands."[2]

Except for the cost of support of aged parents, a responsibility largely taken over by Social Security, the passage could have been written today. Even with the inducement of 401(k)s and other tax-favored savings vehicles, today's workers face the same challenges of saving for one's own retirement as those described in the above passage, written three-quarters of a century ago.

Prior to Social Security, those unable to work routinely moved in with their children. Those who had no children or whose children were unable or unwilling to support them typically wound up in the poorhouse. The poorhouse was not some Dickensian invention; it was an all-too-real means of subsistence for the elderly in the world immediately preceding the enactment of Social Security.

When Social Security became law, every state but New Mexico had poorhouses (sometimes called almshouses or poor farms). The vast majority of the residents were elderly. Most of the "inmates," as they were often labeled, entered the poorhouse late in life, having been independent wage earners until that point. A Massachusetts Commission reporting in 1910 found, for example, that only one percent of the residents had entered the almshouse before the age of 40 while 92 percent entered after age 60.

The poorhouse was a fate to be dreaded, the conditions generally abysmal. Fear of the poorhouse was always lurking in the background, haunting people as they aged. It was a powerful, ubiquitous image in the general culture. The early Monopoly boards, beginning with the game's invention, patented in 1904 as the Landlord's Game, contained a square labeled "Poorhouse." According to the rules, players were sent there when they couldn't meet their expenses. Today, in a world with Social Security, Monopoly boards no longer have a square labeled "Poorhouse." Instead, that same, exact square reads, "Free Parking."

Poorhouses and destitute senior citizens were a fact of life well before the Great Depression. In 1934, the Committee on Economic Security, the inter-Cabinet group appointed by President Franklin

D. Roosevelt to draft a Social Security bill and chaired by Secretary of Labor Frances Perkins, canvassed the available statistics. No national figures existed, but using what was available, the committee reported, "Connecticut (1932), New York (1929), and Wisconsin (1925) found that nearly 50 percent of their aged population (65 years of age and over) had less than subsistence income."[3] In contrast, the poverty rate among the elderly in 2009 was 8.9 percent.

The reduction in the poverty rate of the elderly is directly due to Social Security. According to a 2005 report of the Center for Budget and Policy Priorities, a nonprofit, nonpartisan research organization, "Leaving aside Social Security income, nearly one of every two elderly people—46.8 percent—has income below the poverty line."[4] The percentage is strikingly similar to the poverty rate found before the enactment of Social Security.

Today, almost two-thirds of the elderly receive half or more of their income from Social Security. More than a third receive 90 percent or more of their income from Social Security. The benefits are particularly important to women and minorities. Around half of all unmarried (including widowed) women, African Americans, and Hispanics, aged 65 and older, receive 90 percent or more of their income from Social Security.

Social Security has transformed the lives of younger people as well, as the following story illustrates. On October 17, 1906, Adam Rogalas, a Russian immigrant working at the Iron City Grain Elevator Company in Pittsburgh, Pennsylvania, was suddenly killed when the supports of the floor above gave way, dumping heavy sacks of stored grain on him. He left behind his pregnant wife and four young children. After the accident, Mrs. Rogalas fed her five children by taking in laundry and begging on Sundays in front of the local church. The only assistance the government provided were a few groceries, valued at $6.00 a month, almost nothing for such a large family. Today, Mrs. Rogalas and her children would have received Social Security, just as the families of the victims of 9/11 did and as the families of other workers who suffer disability or death.

As a result of its dependent benefits, Social Security is the nation's largest and most generous children's program. Over 3 million children receive benefits as dependents of workers who have died, become disabled, or retired. More than an additional 3 million children live in families where another member of the household receives Social Security benefits. Thus, about 6.5 million American children—almost 9 percent of all American children—are supported by Social Security benefits. The program is of particular importance to children in low-income families. The children receiving Social Security dependent benefits live in families whose total income is, on average, 25 percent lower than the average for all American families with children. The benefits are also especially important to minority children. For example, because African-Americans have higher rates of disability and premature death than whites, African-American children receive a disproportionate percentage of Social Security's dependent benefits. African-American children constitute 12 percent of all U.S. children under age 18, but represent 21 percent of all children receiving Social Security.

It is the nation's largest and most generous disability program. Monthly Social Security benefits are received by 6.4 million disabled workers. Without that monthly check, 55 percent of disabled workers and their families would live in poverty. Long-term disability is an uncommon private sector benefit. Around 70 percent of the private sector workforce is without it. For nonmanagement and nonprofessional workers, the percentage lacking employer-provided disability insurance is closer to 90 percent.

A median income worker with a spouse and two young children has life insurance and disability insurance with a present value of around $450,000. Although not generally recognized as such, Social Security is often the largest asset that workers and their families have.

Those benefits lift 19.8 million people out of poverty, including over a million children. As important as that is, the transformation of the nation has been about much more than alleviating poverty. Seniors, workers who have become disabled, and families who have lost a breadwinner are no longer left totally destitute, dependent on relatives, private charity, or a government handout. The transformation has been about much more than money. It is about dignity, independence, and freedom.

President Franklin D. Roosevelt was determined to create a program of insurance, rather than what he saw as the dreaded British dole. This was a long-standing concern of the President. In 1931, in his annual message to the legislature, then-Governor Roosevelt stated that the welfare bill enacted in the prior session "may be justified only as a means intended to replace to a large extent the existing methods of poorhouse and poor farm relief," but it should not be expanded, for to do so would "smack of the...dole." Rather, he continued, "Our American aged do not want charity, but rather old age comforts to which they are rightfully entitled by their own thrift and foresight in the form of insurance."

He believed that "the next step to be taken should be based on the theory of insurance by a system of contributions commencing at an early age. In this way," he explained, "men and women will, on arriving at a period when work is no longer practicable, be assured not merely of a roof overhead and enough food to keep body and soul together, but also enough income to maintain life during the balance of their days in accordance with the American standard of living."[5]

In a fireside chat explaining his plan for Social Security, President Roosevelt conceptualized the program as self-help, where Americans were "to use the agencies of government to assist in the establishment of means to provide sound and adequate protection against the vicissitudes of modern life—in other words, social insurance."[6]

Today, some view Social Security as simply a government spending program, undifferentiated from other federal spending, and the deductions from wages that support the program as merely a tax. In keeping with President Roosevelt's vision though, Social Security provides insurance—life insurance, disability insurance, and old age annuities.

Though Social Security is sometimes described as part of the social welfare system, insurance and welfare are intrinsically different, having developed from two very different and distinct historical roots. The antecedents to modern welfare programs can be traced from biblical prescriptions to care for the poor. In contrast, a second, equally rich, but fundamentally different tradition of providing economic security came in the form of a pooling of resources and risk among equals.

Welfare, by definition, provides a benefit based on need. It generally involves an arrangement between financially unequal parties—those materially better off providing assistance to those less advantaged, the poor. The benefit is generally an amount designed to provide the recipient with just enough to get by, as judged by the provider. Eligibility is determined by an examination of the potential recipient's income and assets to ensure that he or she is really in need. Past earnings are irrelevant as long as the person has no accumulated assets. Obviously, if the potential recipient is earning income above the subsistence level, he or she is not in need of the community's help. Moreover, if the person has savings upon which to draw, he or she is, again, not in need of the assistance of others.

In contrast, insurance is a matter of right for those who are eligible. Eligibility is based on achieving insured status, irrespective of need. Welfare programs are designed for people who are already poor. Social insurance prevents workers from becoming poor in the first place. Welfare programs are essential as long as there is poverty, but they have inescapable, inherent weaknesses.

For those people who can earn no more than the community-determined subsistence level, means-tested welfare removes financial incentives to work. Wages reduce the means-tested assistance, leaving recipients where they began. Further, welfare discourages savings. If potential recipients must exhaust their savings before they are eligible to receive welfare, they are penalized for their thrift.

Insurance has none of these shortcomings. If the insurance is designed to replace wages, as Social Security is, work is encouraged. Under Social Security and other wage-replacement pensions, the higher one's prior earnings, the higher the benefit received. Moreover, if the retirement program does not pay fully adequate benefits but simply provides a base on which to build, as Social Security does, it encourages savings. Unlike welfare, savings do not disqualify a person from receipt of benefits. Rather, they permit an additional source of income from which to draw when one is no longer receiving a paycheck.

By definition, then, welfare discourages work; wage-related insurance encourages it. Welfare discourages savings; insurance providing a floor of protection encourages workers to save. To qualify for welfare, recipients must prove something negative about themselves—that they do not have enough to get along on their own. In contrast, beneficiaries of insurance must prove something positive—that they have worked long enough to qualify for benefits.

President Roosevelt's commitment to structuring Social Security as insurance, not welfare, strong as it was, did not emerge as the result of an intellectual exercise and deep study of the objective advantages of insurance over welfare. Rather, Roosevelt preferred insurance because he understood what it meant to be dependent.

Frances Perkins, President Roosevelt's Secretary of Labor and long-time associate, witnessed Roosevelt, who had suffered a polio attack that left him disabled, undergo "a spiritual transformation during the years of his illness . . . The man emerged completely warmhearted, with humility of spirit and with a deeper philosophy. Having been in the depths of trouble, he understood the problems of people in trouble." Roosevelt understood clearly that people would be uplifted in spirit if they worked hard and joined together to provide a common pool of funds from which to draw when working days were over. He understood how demeaning it was for people to have to prove to some other person that they could not support themselves without help, and how crippling in spirit to feel oneself to be helpless and a failure.

President Roosevelt recognized that to get immediate assistance to people in need—to alleviate the immediate suffering caused by the Depression—there was no alternative to welfare. But for the long term—once the Depression was history and the economic health of the country was restored—the President wanted a system of insurance in place to guarantee for posterity that people would have a reliable, stable source of income from which they could draw in old age. Acutely conscious of the debilitating quality of fear, he wanted all workers to have the peace of mind and security that they would be insured against their dependency on wages.

Social Security has eradicated what once was a primary anxiety of the vast majority of workers, the terror of growing old. A writer in 1912 described the attitude people used to have about growing old:

> After the age of sixty has been reached, the transition from non-dependence to dependence is an easy stage—property gone, friends passed away or removed, relatives become few, ambition collapsed, only a few short years left to live, with death a final and welcome end to it all—such conclusions inevitably sweep the wage-earners from the class of hopeful independent citizens into that of the helpless poor.[7]

That world, one of poorhouses and moving in with one's children, has been replaced by an era of financial independence and dignity in old age. Conservatives who have opposed Social Security from the start claim that Social Security curtails personal freedom. In fact, it does the opposite.

People who have independent income have more freedom, not less.

Social Security beneficiaries have the freedom from worry that comes with a stable source of guaranteed income. Independence and financial security in the aftermath of misfortune and in old age are blessings that exist today because of Social Security.

The program is overwhelmingly popular with the American people who understand its great value. It has stood the test of time, transforming the nation in important and magnificent ways.

MY FATHER died in a farming accident when I was only 8 and my brother was 12. Our mom took a job as a waitress to help make ends meet. My brother and I also got odd jobs after school. We took the small amount of money from my father's life insurance and bought a small home in a little town.

Without the help of Social Security benefits (survivors benefits), we would not have been able to make it the first few years after his death. I continued to "draw Social Security" until the maximum age and later was able to go on to college after high school.

I worked my way through school and went on to graduate school and got a degree in health care administration. It has always been fulfilling helping others. My family and I will always be grateful for the monthly benefit check, which helped us through a very tough financial and emotional time in our lives.

— KENNETH HUDSON —
CINCINNATI, OHIO

Framing Social Security for the Twenty-First Century

ERIC R. KINGSON

Eric R. Kingson is a professor of social work at Syracuse
University. He is also co-director of Social Security
Works and co-chair of the Strengthen Social Security
Campaign. He has served as a policy advisor to two
presidential commissions—the 1982–1983 National
Commission on Social Security Reform and the 1994
Bipartisan Commission on Entitlement and Tax
Reform—and as a member of the advisory committee
to the Obama Administration's Social Security
transition team. When Eric was 13, his father died of
cancer, leaving his wife a 41-year-old widow with two
teenagers. Social Security survivors benefits helped
cushion the family against the financial blow. His

mother remarried, but after she became a widow again,
her financial situation changed and, as she got older,
Social Security became an important part of her income.
Eric married and had two children with his wife, Joan,
a professor of child development. In 1998, at age 47,
Joan was diagnosed with stage 4 colon cancer. She was
unable to work and began receiving disability insurance
benefits, which they needed because of the burden of the
heavy medical expenses they incurred. Joan died in May
2001, and their 16-year-old daughter received survivors
benefits until she graduated from high school at age 18.

Our task of reconstruction does not require the creation of new and strange values. It is rather the finding of the way once more to known, but to some degree forgotten, ideals and values. If the means and details are in some instances new, the objectives are as permanent as human nature. Among our objectives I place the security of the men, women, and children of the Nation first. This security for the individual and for the family concerns itself primarily with three factors. People want decent homes to live in; they want to locate them where they can engage in productive work; and they want some safeguard against misfortunes, which cannot be wholly eliminated in this man-made world of ours . . . [S]ecurity was attained in the earlier days through the interdependence of members of families upon each other and of the families within a small community upon each other. The complexities of great communities and of organized industry make less real these simple means of security. Therefore, we are compelled to employ the active interest of the Nation as a whole through government in order to encourage a greater security for each individual who composes it.

—Franklin Delano Roosevelt, June 8, 1934

*A*lthough couched largely in terms of economics, today, the debate over the future of Social Security is most fundamentally a debate about the role of government and the societal values the nation seeks to achieve through Social Security.

This essay begins with a discussion of the understandings, values, and positive social insurance frame giving rise to and structuring Social Security for much of the past 75 years. This traditional Social Security framework, once dominant, has in recent years been challenged largely by a conservative critique that has drawn attention away from Social Security's core goal of providing widespread protection to individuals, families, and the national community against risks to which all are subject. Further, this new frame, the "entitlements problem" framework, defines the contemporary debate almost exclusively in terms of affordability, solvency, and deficit reduction. It pulls attention away from other critical concerns, including improved adequacy of benefits especially for those at great risk, replacement income for family leaves, and benefits for spouses and their dependents or partners, married and not, in Lesbian/Gay/Bisexual/Transgendered families.

The essay concludes by suggesting that those seeking to advance progressive Social Security reform should give greater consideration to developing a narrative, frame, strategies, and policy proposals that reflect the "ideals and values" outlined above in President Franklin Roosevelt's June 8, 1934, message to Congress. Absent this, we are doomed to remain in a defensive posture.

VISION AND VALUES FOR THE FIRST 75 YEARS: THE TRADITIONAL SOCIAL SECURITY FRAME

Frances Perkins, President Roosevelt's Secretary of Labor and chairwoman of the committee that planned the Social Security Act of 1935, spoke of how America had "evolved the ethical principle that it was not right or just that an honest and industrious man should live and die in misery" (1934). The New Deal, and by extension, Social Security, she said, elsewhere, was based on "an attitude that found voice in expressions like 'the people are what matter to government,' and 'a government should aim to give all the people under its jurisdiction the best possible life.'" Princeton economist and Provost J. Douglas Brown (1898–1986), also an architect of the Social Security Act, spoke eloquently of an implied covenant in Social Security, arising from a deeply embedded sense of mutual responsibility in civilization. This covenant, he wrote, underlies the fundamental obligation of the government and citizens of one time and the government and citizens of another time to maintain a contributory social insurance system."

Thus, it is not surprising that from its inception, Social Security has given expression to and reinforced widely held values, including reward for hard work; the responsibility to care for parents, family, self, and neighbors; respect for the dignity of every person; use of government to help individuals and families do for themselves what they cannot do alone.

A practical solution to risks to the economic security of workers and their families, Social Security reflects the solidarity across generations, which is integral to a well-functioning society. An embodiment of this interdependence, Social Security unites generations through its support of older Americans, severely disabled workers and their families, and family members surviving the death of a parent or spouse. Emerging from and fortifying this necessary interdependence among people, sectors, and generations, Social Security balances individualism with an understanding that individuals thrive in the context of families and communities; that we, as a people, bear risk and all have obligations to each other.

By doing so, Social Security provides one "solution" to the risks posed by three major life events—death of a parent or spouse, old age, and disabling conditions. All people and all societies address such risks through a variety of private and public mechanisms. Individuals and families often bear these risks themselves or by caring for and supporting family members experiencing major difficulties. Private insurance and employer-based benefits provide protection as do a number of public mechanisms including, for example, mandates for individuals to purchase health insurance; mandates or incentives to employers to provide protections; welfare programs such as Supplemental Security Income and Medicaid.

Social insurance, the approach to economic security that drives Social Security, protects against identifiable risks that could overwhelm the finances of individuals and their families. Where welfare programs seek to relieve extreme financial problems, social insurance programs seek to prevent financial distress. Built on the principle of universal coverage, social insurance provides a social means of pooling risks. In exchange for making relatively modest work-related contributions over many years, social insurance provides individuals and their families with a floor of protection against predictable risk.

"Social adequacy"—that benefits should meet the basic needs of the protected population—is Social Security's driving principle. Absent a concern to provide widespread, adequate financial protection, there would be little reason for Social Security and other social insurance programs; protection against identified risks could be left to families and other private mechanisms (e.g., private savings).

Although less important, "individual equity"—that benefits should reflect prior contributions and that the more one contributes the larger benefit returns should be—also influences the structure of social insurance programs. That is why, under Social Security, people who have worked consistently at higher wages—making larger payroll tax contributions into the program—receive larger monthly benefits. However, reflecting the adequacy principle, Social Security's progressive benefit formula assures that benefits replace a substantially larger portion of preretirement earnings for low- and moderate-income workers.

Of necessity, Social Security is also conservatively financed and monitored. Payroll tax contributions, income from taxing Social Security benefits, and interest earned on Treasury notes flow to Social Security's trust funds, earmarked to pay for benefits and program costs. Many safeguards assure stable financing. Legislative oversight, annual reports by program officials, review by actuaries and independent panels of experts provide an early warning system for financing problems that will arise from time to time. The authority and taxing power of government as well as the self-interest of political leaders and the public to protect promised benefits guarantee the continuity and financial integrity of Social Security.

THE EMERGENCE OF THE "ENTITLEMENTS PROBLEM" FRAME

Social Security is the nation's most successful and popular program, the "poster child" for government working well on behalf of the American people. Seamlessly and efficiently (i.e., only one percent of its expenditures are for administration!), it provides benefits each month to over 54 million Americans (including 4.4 million children) and covers nearly all against lost wages arising from death or disability or retirement of a worker.

Even so, Social Security was and continues to be challenged by those believing it an unwarranted extension of federal power. At first, it was attacked as "socialistic." Nevertheless, from the early 1950s through the mid-1970s, a strong favorable consensus combined with a growing economy and the need to improve benefits to fuel the incremental expansion of the program. By the early 1950s, it was so much a part of the nation's fabric that Republican President Dwight Eisenhower wrote to his brother in 1954 that:

Should any political party attempt to abolish social security, unemployment insurance, and eliminate labor laws and farm programs, you would not hear of that party again in our political history. There is a tiny splinter group, of course, that believes you can do these things. Among them are . . . a few . . . Texas oil millionaires, and an occasional politician or businessman from other areas. Their number is negligible and they are stupid.

Later in 1956, President Eisenhower signed amendments adding disability insurance protections to Social Security.

Even as the "easy votes" on Social Security came to an end, bipartisan support was found in 1977 and 1983 for a combination of revenue increases and benefit reductions that ultimately cured Social Security's funding for half a century.

But before the ink was dry on the 1983 financing amendments, new and creative attacks emerged.

Writing in 1983 in the journal of the libertarian Cato Institute, Stuart Butler, vice-president of the Heritage Foundation, and Peter Germanis, then an analyst with the Heritage Foundation, advanced a tongue-in-cheek "Leninist strategy" to deconstruct Social Security. Calling for "guerrilla warfare against the current social security system and the coalition that supports it," they suggested that radical conservative advocates should: 1) assure existing beneficiaries and older workers that new proposals would not harm them; 2) demonstrate flaws in and disadvantages of the current program; 3) develop a credible privatized alternative; 4) sell this alternative as beneficial to the young, most of whom question Social Security's future; and (5) engage powerful private interest groups (e.g., financial industry) that stand to gain from privatization.

Concurrently, the advocates of shrinking social spending made "good" use of hyperbole and crises, real and constructed, to advance their agenda. By the mid-1980s, a new political theme, "Generational Equity," emerged as a catchall slogan. The concept asserted that 1) support of policies for elderly persons was a major cause of growing federal deficits; 2) elderly persons received too large a portion of social welfare spending to the detriment of children and other groups; 3) the projected future growth in the costs of these programs would place an unsustainable burden on future workers; 4) younger people would not receive fair returns on their Social Security investments; and 5) all of these factors, if left unchecked, would lead to generational conflict.

Variations on this theme pronounced Social Security unfair to the poor because it did not end poverty, unfair to the rich because they did not get the same rate of return as the poor, unfair to African-Americans, Latinos, and women.

Former Governor Richard D. Lamm put it this way in 1985:

> Simply put, America's elderly have become an intolerable burden on the economic system and the younger generation's future. In the name of compassion for the elderly, we have handcuffed the young, mortgaged their future, and drastically limited their hopes and aspirations.

By the mid-1990s, Social Security was being recast as part of an "entitlement crisis." Conservatives were rewriting the Social Security narrative and, reframing the debate, around their preferred values— small government, privatization, personal responsibility, and President George W. Bush's "ownership society." Republican pollster Frank Luntz was advising Republican members of the House of Representatives in 1995 to frame the budget debate "in terms of 'the American dream' and 'our children's future.'" Turn "the issue of 'fairness' against the Democrats," he argued, by asking, "Is it 'fair' for Medicare recipients to have an even greater choice of doctors and facilities than the average taxpayers who are funding the system?" On cue, the Bipartisan Commission on Entitlement and Tax Reform (1995) warned that entitlement spending will "unfairly burden America's children and [stifle] standards of living for this and future generations."

By 2001, radical changes long rejected by liberals, moderates, and most conservatives—such as privatizing, means-testing, and otherwise greatly reducing protections—had gradually been legitimated. Having just won the 2004 presidential election, President George W. Bush declared he had "capital to spend" and he used it to launch his effort to partially privatize Social Security. Although privatization proposals were, with much effort, rebuffed, this full-scale assault placed the traditional supporters of Social Security on the defensive. Relatively little attention could be given to promoting a progressive Social Security strategy.

Ironically, even with the 2008 election of Barack Obama as President and a Democratic House and Senate, there has been no letup of the attacks on Social Security. If anything, Social Security's landscape is more difficult to negotiate. The Peter G. Peterson Foundation, drawing on a billion dollar contribution by its namesake, is funding numerous efforts to propagate this perspective, an important reason why today the conservative "entitlements problem" frame has found considerable support across party lines and has influenced the thinking and stance of many, including President Obama. With the executive order that established the National Commission on Fiscal Responsibility and Reform and with his appointments to the commission, the President clearly signaled retreat from advancing an economic investment and jobs strategy and a willingness to engage significant cuts in Social Security.

As Nancy Altman and I have written elsewhere, notwithstanding claims that the goal is to protect "our grandchildren" and future generations, the commission represents a continuation of "the Reagan Administration's "starve the beast" strategy and the deficit politics that have driven domestic policy since the early 1980s. . . . Tax increases and defense cuts—other than those affecting the pay and benefits of our servicemen and women, veterans and their families—have mostly been off the table." The commission has effectively institutionalized the conservative frame on "entitlements" and, this framing invites competition over resources among deserving populations and their representatives. Adding injury to irony, some members of the commission, including Democratic Senator Kent Conrad and Republican Congressman Paul Ryan, insist in equally self-righteous tones that the Bush tax cuts for the very rich must be continued even as they call for cuts in Social Security.

POLICIES AND A BROADENED POLICY FRAME FOR THE TWENTY-FIRST CENTURY

The Great Recession has destabilized the finances of many families, including people nearing retirement. Occupational pensions offer less protection to working persons today. Housing prices and retirement savings have nose-dived for many. And the Center for Retirement Research at Boston College recently released a study in September of 2010 identifying a $6.6 trillion gap between what Americans are saving today and what they need to save to maintain their standard of living in retirement.

The one good retirement story through all of this is Social Security. The program is working as intended. Benefits are paid out in full and, under the most widely accepted estimates, can be through 2036. If successive Congresses and presidential administrations chose to do nothing before then (a most unlikely scenario), there would still be a dedicated stream of income from payroll tax contributions of workers and their employers, sufficient to pay 75 cents on every dollar that is promised. Obviously, this is a problem, but it is nothing to panic about. To put this in perspective, the projected shortfall is roughly equivalent to what it would cost to extend the Bush tax cuts to the upper 2 percent of income earners. Yet another parallel, asking employees and employers to make payroll tax contributions on all earnings in excess of $106,800, would provide sufficient income to fully address the projected shortfall past 2084.

Remarkably, in the midst of the nation's halting economic recovery, most politicians, journalists, and other policy elites seem to have convinced themselves that Social Security protections must be reduced. It doesn't seem to matter that public opinion polls consistently show that there is no support for cutting Social Security and that Social Security is one area where the public mostly supports tax increases as an alternative to benefit cuts. The elites know best!

With rare exception, the suggestion that serious consideration should be given to expanding, not cutting, Social Security protections is met with quizzical looks or mere silence. A few small (and potentially useful) targeted changes are on the agenda, but mostly because they are seen as the sweeteners necessary to cut the bitter taste of the serious cuts that are being "teed up."

But the facts are that benefits, though secure, are modest by any standard, averaging about $1,200 a month for retirees and $1,100 for all others. Millions of Social Security beneficiaries have had little choice but to accept reduced early retirement benefits because they could no longer find or did not have sufficient health to continue in their work. The recession is further adding to their numbers. The giving of care to family members, mainly by women, reduces the protections of these caregivers. Disability applicants face huge processing delays, and if they receive benefits, they still must wait 24 months before they are eligible for Medicare. Benefits for children whose households have lost income due to the death, disability, and in a few cases the retirement of a parent, were once available through age 21 if the young person was involved in completing vocational or college education, but today stop at age 18. Unlike many other nations, the United States does not provide paid family leave, neither does it provide long-term care protections under its social insurance programs. And discrimination continues against lesbian, gay, bisexual, and transgender persons and their family members.

Plainly, much can be done to improve the nation's Social Security program. And, with time, thought, and planning, much will done.

In closing I would like to suggest that several points should be considered for those interested in advancing a progressive Social Security agenda for the next 75 years:

DEFENSE IS IMPORTANT. To begin to secure Social Security for the twenty-first century, we must block counterproductive proposals that would diminish the nation's, really the people's, Social Security.

BY DEFINITION, DEFENSE WON'T GET US VERY FAR. Long term, even if we win some battles, absent a positive agenda, we will lose.

THOSE WHO FRAME THE DEBATE USUALLY WIN. Conservatives have been persistent and smart in advancing their "generational equity" theme and "entitlement problem" framework. We, in turn, need to give thought to developing our themes and frame.

VALUES MATTER. We need to give careful thought to values we want to achieve and to a vision that communicates the Social Security story and connects to the public's experience and beliefs. When we do, we should remember President Roosevelt's earlier words that the "task does not require the creation of new and strange values [but] rather the finding of the way once more to known, but to some degree forgotten, ideals and values" (very possibly including collective responsibility and interdependence).

Reverend Jim Wallis, president and CEO of the Sojourners, begins his book, *Rediscovering Values* (2010) by observing that:

The 2008–2009 economic crisis presents us with an enormous opportunity: to rediscover our values—as people, as families, as communities of faith, and as a nation. It is a moment we dare not pass by. We have forgotten some very important things, and it is time to remember them again. Yes, we do need an economic recovery, but we also need a moral recovery—on Wall Street, Main Street, and Your Street . . .

An affirmative and practical Social Security agenda that appeals to our "better angels" can and should be an important part of this moral recovery.

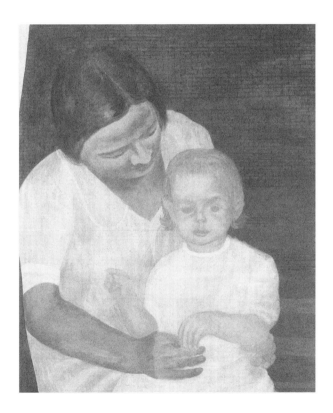

I AM A PROUD and happy Social Security recipient (along with my husband). Social Security saved us—I retired in late 2006; in June of 2008 we were flooded out of our home of 27 years and I had major surgery. Social Security truly came to our rescue, because my pension wasn't great.

— ROBERTA TILL-RETZ —
IOWA CITY, IOWA

Social Security and the Current Pension Crisis

Teresa Ghilarducci

All her adult life, Teresa Ghilarducci has worked on
the issue of retirement security on the voluntary level,
to which mandatory Social Security provides the base.
A labor economist and a leading national authority on
issues related to retirement security and the current
pension crisis, she is the Bernard L. and Irene Schwartz
Chair in economic policy and analysis at the New
School. Her most recent book, *When I'm Sixty-Four:
The Plot Against Pensions and the Plan to Save Them*,
describes the current loss or reduction of pension
income for senior citizens and proposes a system of
Guaranteed Retirement Accounts to supplement Social
Security, an idea that has gained major recognition from
policy planners.

*S*ocial Security is the major source of income for most elderly Americans but, for the first time in two generations, retirement income security for people approaching retirement age will be worse than that of their parents and grandparents. Social Security replacement rates are falling because Medicare premiums are increasing. At the same time, employer-sponsored pensions—designed to supplement Social Security—have eroded partly because Congress, employers, and the money management industry promoted 401(k)-type plans at the expense of the expanding traditional pensions. Thus for a younger generation, two of the three tiers of the retirement income security pyramid are eroding.

In this financial crisis, and the ones that will follow, Social Security emerges as the base of retirement income support. Why? It is because its value doesn't fluctuate with financial markets. But the two smaller layers in the retirement income pyramid—the employer pension system that provides the middle tier and personal assets that form the tip—flip-flop and dive, when property, bond, and stock markets collapse or bubble. Between 2008 and 2010, people lost 25 percent of their pension and personal assets, and even more if the decimation of home equity is included. Social Security is the only reliable guaranteed benefit for the growing number of people without pensions and even those with pensions. But it is not enough to prevent poverty and drastic declines in living standards in old age.

Therefore, universal retirement security is our next hurdle to protect working families and an aging population. We need a universal guaranteed tier of pension income to supplement Social Security, a fresh option that can compete with the high fee and high-risk commercial and individual directed 401(k) system.

Let us pause now and not lose sight of our successes. One of the hallmarks of the American system of social insurance—which include generous tax breaks, employer pension plans, disability, and Social Security—is that working people, rich and poor alike, can afford to retire.

Indeed, that the rich and poor can have a healthy period of old age leisure is the success of a civilized society.

That is why people care so much. The upcoming retirement crises may be one of several areas where "the people" are ahead of the politicians. Recent polls, for example by McKinsey & Company, show that people want the government to guarantee retirement income. They rank retirement more highly than government progress on jobs, which is shocking in a great recession. It should be especially telling for politicians that the people most likely to vote—higher income people and whites—are more anxious about their retirement future and fear "things" are going to get worse, than are lower income people and minorities.

Fear explains the polls. Americans are scared about their retirement. In a recent Gallup poll of people ages 44 to 75, more than 90 percent said we are facing a retirement crisis, and 61 percent said they fear depleting their assets *more than they fear dying.*

In addition, for the first time since Gallup conducted the survey in 1995, the number of individuals planning to work beyond 65 now outnumbers those who are planning to retire before that age. Yet, this desire may only be a wish, dissonant with reality. Sadly, during the worst recession since the Great Depression, the unemployment rates for older workers are increasing the fastest. Whether to work or not is not in the sole control of older people.

There is much opportunity in Americans' concern about their retirement insecurity, but first let's turn to the foundation of the insecurity.

EROSION IN RETIREMENT ADEQUACY

According to the Center for Retirement Research at Boston College a growing share of working-age households are at risk of being unable to maintain their preretirement standard of living in retirement. The Center for Retirement Research estimates that 51 percent of households will likely not have enough income to maintain their living standards in retirement. If health care and long-term care costs are included, the share of households "at risk" increases to 65 percent.

The old consensus about adequacy was that the percentage of preretirement income needed in retirement to maintain living standards varies with income because higher income workers pay a higher percentage of preretirement income in work-related expenses—especially in taxes and saving for retirement. So that high-income individuals—defined here as the top 20 percent—need a lower replacement rate than lower income workers (defined as the bottom 40 percent). There is a consensus of opinion that lower income workers need more income in retirement than while they were working because their preretirement income was at the poverty level. Lower income workers should have replacement rates higher than 100 percent of preretirement pay. There is some support to raise incomes of the very poor and very old—this group is among the most "deserving poor"—but the responsibility for this group is generally out of the hands of employer pensions.

For middle-class workers, 80 percent of preretirement income is the standard. Since people have more time in retirement, it is assumed that they will replace expensive activities with time-intensive activities, such as preparing more home-cooked meals.

However, the presumption that people need less income in retirement has been challenged by the fact that uninsured health costs are higher in retirement and over half of the elderly are retiring with mortgages. Therefore, there is an emerging new consensus that middle- and high-income people need close to 95 percent to 100 percent of income to maintain living standards because more elderly are in debt.

Higher income white males have enjoyed the largest increases in longevity: the use of statin drugs and reduction in cigarette smoking are key factors.

There is also concern that longevity improvements will decline with increases in obesity and disorders related to obesity.

Overall, longevity for 65 year olds has increased approximately 25 percent since 1950; the economy (or gross domestic product per capita) has increased 244 percent. Overall time spent in retirement has increased as employer pensions and Social Security have expanded. Society has chosen to use the increases in prosperity to increase retirement time.

The upshot of this is that people need to save more. The Aon Consulting Group has been analyzing the needs of retirees since its first report for the President's Commission on Pension Policy in 1980. The plain math is that, in order to replace working income for retirement, people should save about 17 percent to 20 percent of their income. Let's count Social Security for 12 percent of that goal; people thus need to save an extra 8 percent every pay period. Hardly anyone does. And if they do they are likely to withdraw it during times of economic stress. Aon shows that people earning $30,000 to $90,000 per year who are 50 to 64 years old save between 2.79 percent and 5.57 percent of their income. Given the assets that people in this age group have, they should be saving, in some retirement vehicle, 33 percent to 45 percent. If they saved since they were 25 years old, consistently for the past 30 years, they would be fine at that savings rate.

If people save continuously starting at age 25, only the highest income earners come close to saving enough for retirement. In sum, the rise of the 401(k) system has given rise to a paradox. The institutions that are meant to help people save have been coincident with a dramatic decrease in retirement savings.

FAILED INSTITUTIONS

Over the past 30 years, workplace pensions—which only covered about 50 percent of the workforce—have changed form in a crucial way. Defined benefit plans (DBs) have been retrenched or terminated and have been replaced with 401(k)-type plans called defined contribution plans (DCs). New, large firms are only offering DC plans. Public employees are the only sector where DBs are prevalent.

Why did employer pensions disappear? The reason is not because workers did not want them; the observed popularity of 401(k) plans is mostly a "second best" phenomenon. People consider 401(k) plans simply to be better than nothing.

One way to see why DCs are second best is to imagine what would happen to pension security if one third of public pension plans switched to a DC system and all private employers froze their DB plans. Over one out of four people retiring in the next 15 to 20 years (people called the "last wave boomers" because they were born at the end of the baby boom between 1956–1965) will have lower family incomes than they otherwise would have had at age 67. Also, the predictions are that if there is a big move to DC plans from DB plans, only 11 percent of "the last wave boomers" will see their incomes increase (and most of the income gains will be under 5 percent). And those gains will not be real gains since they will be accompanied by more assumption of risk.

Another way that DC plans are second best is that workers do worse under DC plans because employers contribute less money to pensions when employers make the switch. When employers switch to DC plans, expenses fall and smaller pension fund amounts are accumulated.

Let's face it. Voluntary, commercial pension institutions have failed. Over the past 30 years, private employers have experimented with 401(k)-type plans, which have lowered employers' expenses according to the Towers Watson report in 2009. As sure as night follows day, pension savings accumulations have been eroded. Employers have stopped and started contributions and have varied their matches. Firms who handle 401(k) plans' assets admit their business models focus on the top earners.

Congress made matters worse by encouraging, through tax breaks that come in the form of a tax deduction, 401(k) plans that serve primarily high-income households at the expense of middle- and low-income workers.

According to the Economic Policy Institute's Ross Eisenbrey, if the tax breaks for 401(k)s and IRAs were reduced or eliminated, the top one percent would shoulder 48 percent of the subsidy loss, and general revenues would increase by over $100 billion to spend on more retirement plans, or youth programs or bridges to somewhere. Len Burman and colleagues in 2004 and 2009, at the Urban-Brookings Tax Policy Center, estimated that 80 percent of the tax subsidies for retirement savings have gone to the top 20 percent of earners. As Eisenbrey colorfully says, "This is government welfare stood on its head." There is no rationale for providing a larger tax break to a millionaire than to a Wal-Mart cashier for the same dollar contribution to a 401(k) plan (and nothing at all if the cashier owes payroll but not income tax). Similarly, high earners receive more help from employers, who contribute 5 percent of earnings, on average, to the retirement accounts of households in the 75th percentile, compared with less than 2 percent for those at the 25th percentile, according to the Congressional Research Service.

About half of American workers have such plans and their average value is just $60,000 and, of course, are dependent on the roller coaster of the market and subject to the fees charged by fund managers.

After 32 years and trillions in tax subsidies, 401(k) plans have worsened—rather than improved—retirement security because the design of the 401(k) ensures that its tax subsidies go disproportionately to high-income earners while very little goes to low-income earners.

Rather than continue to make this situation worse by increasing the 401(k) contribution limits, which benefits only the highest earners, Congress should restructure the tax subsidies to ensure that they help everyone save for retirement and provide no greater aid to the upper class than to the working class. One common sense improvement would be to change the current system of deductions into tax credits and make them refundable. But that only solves one problem. Comprehensive reform is needed.

There are potential solutions to the retirement crisis, but tweaks and small changes at the margins won't be enough.

SOLUTION

Strengthening Social Security—rather than further weakening it by reducing benefits (such as raising the retirement age or reducing the COLA)—is necessary but not sufficient to restore retirement security. A coalition of unions, senior groups, the liberal Economic Policy Institute, and the nonprofit Pension Rights Center—called Retirement USA—has reached out to employers and the financial industry to construct a set of principles for pension reform. A plan meeting those principles will help individuals save and invest without having their savings worn away by preretirement loans and withdrawals, bad investments, bad and expensive management, and just plain bad luck. A system that relies on tax incentives to induce people to save will always favor high-income workers who can afford to save and would do so without generous tax subsidies. An effective system must be universal and target government subsidies to have the greatest effect and meet the greatest need.

Retirement USA's principles aim to make pensions universal, cost efficient, effective in accumulating assets for adequate pensions, affordable and sustainable, and fair to people in all kinds of jobs. The principles are the following:

1. Employers, employees, and targeted government subsidies all contribute to workers pensions: workers need help saving for retirement.

2. Social Security and employer pensions, together, should provide an adequate income replacement after a full career of working.

3. Hard-earned and accumulated assets should be managed professionally and in a pooled fund so that fees are low and the investment decisions are professional. At present, 401(k) participants must make their own investment decisions and bear the risk of adverse investment performance.

4. Fees must be low. The high fees associated with 401(k) plans can decimate long-term returns. The Center for Retirement Research estimates that net investment returns were a full percentage point higher for defined-benefit pension plans than for 401(k)-type defined contribution plans between 1988 and 2004, despite a lower concentration of funds invested in equities. With compounding of the returns on the investment, this small-sounding difference could translate into a 30 percent larger nest egg at retirement.

5. Government subsidies should go to the people who need it most. 401(k)s and IRAs, in which taxes on earnings are deferred, reduce tax receipts by $193 billion a year. But 80 percent of these tax breaks go to the top 20 percent of taxpayers. Her solution: "Guaranteed Retirement Accounts," to which employers and employees would each be required to contribute 2.5 percent of salaries, with a $600 refundable tax credit for the employee's contribution.

6. The payout is in the form of annuities at retirement. Another key risk—one the Gallup survey identified—is longevity. A real pension guarantees a monthly payment for a lifetime, whereas retirees can and do outlive their 401(k) assets. Every worker is covered and a person's

pension savings should not be lost when changing jobs. One of the biggest hurdles to spurring retirement savings is that half of the nation's workers do not have access to a retirement account through their employer. Many work for small businesses, which often lack resources to navigate the relevant regulations. To help these workers, the federal government should provide "off-the-shelf" options that businesses can offer to workers with limited regulatory burdens.

7. Financial Markets are too risky. Luck plays an oversized role in whether retirement savings in personal accounts will be adequate. Even 401(k) participants who make relatively conservative investment allocation decisions over a longtime horizon are subject to unacceptable risks. Gary Burtless of the Brookings Institution has estimated that 401(k) participants who contributed 4 percent of their wages over 40 years and invested the funds in a portfolio split equally between long-term government bonds and stocks would be able to replace a quarter of their preretirement earnings if they retired in 2008. This replacement rate is only half as much as a similar worker who retired in 1999, but much better than a worker who retired in 1974, who would have a dismal replacement rate of only 18 percent.

I, with colleagues at the Economic Policy Institute, have proposed a plan for Guaranteed Retirement Accounts (GRAs). Employers and employees would each be required to contribute 2.5 percent of salaries, with a $600 refundable tax credit for the employee's contribution into a federally administered cash balance plan. The GRA accounts, which could not be touched until retirement, would be pooled and managed by professionals, as private defined pensions are now managed, with a target of a 3 percent return above the rate of inflation. At the end of a normal working life, the average worker would accumulate, along with Social Security, enough to assure a 70 percent replacement rate of preretirement income.

Guaranteed Retirement Account plans (GRAs) have a similar macroeconomic benefit that Social Security has. Social Security keeps consumption steady while GRAs would keep savings steady. "National savings would get a boost," I wrote in *Bloomberg Businessweek* last July of 2010.

The GRA meets all of the principles the Retirement USA coalition set out as essential to deliver retirement income that is universal, secure, and adequate.

Another popular reform proposal comes from President Obama, which is basically a soft mandate. All employees would be steered into existing 401(k) and IRA accounts. The Auto IRA plan would require employers to enroll workers automatically into a plan, and if there is no plan to put workers in an IRA. The Government Accountability Office reported in the fall of 2009 that auto enrollment increased participation in employer-sponsored plans to as high as 95 percent, but that the savings rates were insufficient for retirement adequacy. There is also evidence that people may accommodate increased savings at work by taking on more debt somewhere else in their portfolio or save less in other ways.

In the auto IRA proposal, policymakers would be attempting to nudge individuals toward saving more. But the nudges are expensive. The plan would add a $50 billion saver's tax credit on top of the $190 billion in tax subsidies for 401(k), IRA, and other retirement accounts.

Retirement needs and expectations are based on social norms and practical considerations. No modern nations have found it practical to make individuals save for their own retirement in individual accounts to fund retirement. If we do, the consequence will be an increase in elderly poverty rates and a continuing decline in living standards for older Americans, many of whom have worked 40 or more years.

NEVER DID I think I would be drawing a Social Security benefit at the early age of 60—I'm a "junior-senior," who is vibrant, active, with many solid work years ahead. But following a state budget crisis and layoff in 2009, with no job in sight, I was forced to accept my deceased ex-husband's Social Security as a survivor benefit. I thank him every day, and I thank Social Security, as it prevented me from going bankrupt, even possibly homeless. I am now seeking permanent part-time work and feel blessed that I have a "cushion" for life. I am not as well off as some, but much better off than others. In a country with increasing haves vs. have-nots, Social Security is, for many, the only soft place to land.

— MARIE BARTLETT —
HENDERSONVILLE, NORTH CAROLINA

Social Security, Medicare, Deficits, and Debt

James K. Galbraith

Economist James Galbraith is a professor at the
University of Texas and author of *The Predator State*.
His father was economist John Kenneth Galbraith,
a professor at Harvard University who served in the
administrations of Franklin Delano Roosevelt and
John F. Kennedy. His parents, Ken and Kitty, received
both Social Security and Medicare. Though his father
earned a good living and they were not reliant on Social
Security, Medicare coverage gave them the assurance
that a medical emergency would not impose an end-of-
life financial burden. Medicare has prevented millions
of families from medical bankruptcy due to end-of-life
expenses.

*I*n recent years we have been subjected to a rising cacophony of nonsense about a looming financial crisis—and the reference is not to the very real meltdown of private financial markets. Rather, we are told, *future unfunded entitlements* will bankrupt our government as the baby boomers retire. Social Security and Medicare are said to be the main source of what former Comptroller General David Walker has called the "super sub-prime crisis."

Social Security and Medicare have always had enemies, closely allied to private insurance companies who would like the business, and to fund managers and others who would profit from privatization of the associated revenue streams. But recently, these enemies have been given a boost, and a claim to respectability, by arguments linking Social Security and Medicare to the larger issues of the national deficit and debt, especially in the long term.

In these arguments, federal government revenue and expenditure streams are compared over very long periods—even over infinite time. "Deficit gaps" are then used to measure the financial burden of these commitments, and therefore the alleged solvency or insolvency of the government. The results, amounting to tens of trillions of dollars, are headline-grabbing and scary-looking. Evidently this combination makes them irresistible, at least to some people.

UNDERSTANDING WHAT THE DEFICIT IS

The federal government spends by cutting checks—or, what is functionally the same thing, by directly crediting private bank accounts. This is a matter of typing numbers into a machine. That is all federal spending is. Unlike private firms, the federal government maintains no stock of cash on hand and no credit balance at the bank. It doesn't need to do so. There are surely limits of wisdom and prudence on federal spending, as well as numerous checks, balances, and self-imposed constraints, but there is no operational limit. The federal government can, and does, spend what it wants.

While it is common to regard government tax revenue as income, this income is not comparable to that of firms or households. Government can choose to exact greater tax revenues by imposing new taxes or raising tax rates. No firm can do this; even firms with market power know that consumers will find substitutes if prices are raised too much. Moreover firms, households, and even state and local governments require income or borrowings in order to spend. The federal government's spending is not constrained by revenues or borrowing. This is a fact, completely noncontroversial, but very poorly understood.

Tax receipts debit bank accounts. So does borrowing from the public. These are operationally distinct from spending. There is no operational procedure through which the federal government "uses" tax receipts or borrowings for its spending. If, perchance, one chooses to pay taxes in cash, the Treasury simply issues a receipt and shreds the cash. It has no need for the income in order to spend. This is why it is a mistake to look at federal tax receipts as an equivalent concept to income of households or firms.

Federal government spending has exceeded tax revenues, with only brief exceptions, since the founding. The budget deficit is just the accounting reflection of this difference. Though the size of the deficit is a reflection of larger economic conditions and policies, it has practically no economic significance on its own. There is no evidence, nor any economic theory, behind the proposition that federal government spending ever needs to match federal government tax receipts—over any period, short or long.

PUBLIC DEBTS ARE PRIVATE ASSET

A statement of "financial condition" is, in general, a balance sheet. These are constructed with two columns: one for liabilities, and the other for assets. This very basic principle is no different for the public sector, and for the nation as a whole, than it is for private sector accounting.

The "nation's financial condition" is a combination of the financial condition of the government and that of its citizens. It is thus necessary to count the assets of the public sector alongside the liabilities of the public sector. Thus, in the real world, we observe that the U.S. federal government tends to run persistent deficits. This is matched by a persistent tendency of the nongovernment sector to save. Debt issued between private parties cancels out; but that between the government and the private sector remains, with the private sector's net financial wealth consisting of the government's net debt.

The obligations of the Social Security system are a long-term public sector liability. But the same obligations are also, of course, a long-term asset to the public. The Social Security wealth of the current population is just as real as the liabilities that support it.

In political discourse, the picture is often confused by treating the forecast difference between Social Security benefits and FICA tax revenues, projected over time and discounted to the present, as a "net liability" of the government. In this way, Social Security's critics purport to show an "unfunded burden" being incurred now, for the benefit of the future retired population. This overlooks the fact that the underlying citizens are the same people: today's workers will become, eventually, tomorrow's retirees. It is hard to see why today's workers should object if the burden of payroll taxes does not, in present value terms, equal the value of Social Security benefits.

Tomorrow's workers might, of course, object to paying out Social Security benefits. But they can hardly care about past payroll tax receipts, which have no bearing on the real burden of supporting the older population in the future. Their only real basis for complaint would be that promised Social Security benefits are too high. Yet, in the real world, there is no evidence that this is so. Indeed, deficit-based objections to Social Security make no such claim, preferring to invent complicated accounting arguments to obscure the fact that future Social Security benefits—like those today—are modest.

WILL THE CAPITAL MARKETS SUPPORT SOCIAL SECURITY?

Many people claim to worry that the burdens of future entitlements will cause problems for the Treasury's efforts to borrow to meet today's needs.

Can we imagine that the U.S. domestic sector will reach a point such that it will refuse to accumulate dollar claims on our government, in the form of currency and interest-bearing government bonds? Would we ever reach the point where American businesses would refuse to sell their wares for U.S. currency? If households or banks had more currency than desired, would they refuse to sell it for Treasuries? If so, that would mean that government spending would be immediately inflationary, as it was in Germany in 1923. These scenarios are intensely improbable, to say the least.

Low long-term interest rates tell us that the markets are not troubled by such possibilities. Nor is it possible for such concerns, should they arise in the markets, to become actual problems, even with the growth of "entitlements" over the next three-quarters of a century. It is not sufficient to show that on some set of assumptions projected tax revenue might fall short of projected spending. Rather, there must be some explanation as to why that should be a matter of concern, why and how borrowing might become difficult or constrained—particularly given that we now have accumulated over two centuries of experience of tax shortfalls with, predictably, no suggestion of government insolvency.

Is there some economic limit to the nominal value of the bonds that can be issued by the U.S. Treasury? The reality is: no such limit exists.

MISUSE OF ECONOMIC PROJECTIONS AND ASSUMPTIONS

It has become a habit for the Social Security actuaries to violate generally accepted accounting practices when making economic projections relevant to the financial flows of the Social Security system. Specifically, past performance is characteristically ignored, and future projections are systematically pessimistic. This has led in recent years to repeated, systematic revisions of the financial projections for Social Security, always in the direction of rolling back the projected dates when benefits exceed payroll taxes and the so-called Trust Fund is exhausted. This pattern has been so systematic, that it is reasonable to conclude that the actuaries have been systematically and persistently pessimistic.

DIVIDING UP THE BUDGET IN ARBITRARY WAYS

Should Social Security and Medicare be segregated in the federal budget at all? The argument in favor has always been political: that the presence of FICA contributions assures that payments will be made. But the "Social Security deficit" argument—however spurious—works in the other direction, toward mandating cuts in these programs. So it is debatable whether discussions of Social Security and Medicare's finances *per se* are constructive, anymore.

As economics, it makes no sense to discuss these programs apart from the larger budget. The purpose of a program budget is to discipline the program. It is to hold managers accountable, and to discourage fraud. However, there is little public interest in reporting long-range projections of the "fiscal balance" of particular portions of the budget. And while officials in any program should be held accountable after the fact, there is little public purpose, and no economic interest, served by reporting the resulting, after-the-fact fiscal balance of particular portions of the federal budget.

Thus, the long-term success of Social Security should not depend on, nor be assessed by, matching spending on that program with some portion of federal tax revenue. The economic effects of budget deficits are the same whether they result from Social Security spending that exceeds payroll tax revenue or from transportation spending that exceeds transportation taxes. If, over time, we should find that projected payroll tax receipts fall significantly short of desired Social Security spending, then it would no longer make sense to adopt a budgeting procedure that dedicates—in a purely planning sense—payroll tax receipts to the Social Security program.

ARBITRARY, CAPRICIOUS, AND MISLEADING TIME HORIZONS

Yet another technique in the entitlement scare campaign concerns time horizons. By projecting events out in time, and by manipulating discount rates, it is possible to make practically any number appear in a net present value calculation.

An example is the assumption of current Medicare forecasts that health care costs will continue to rise indefinitely more rapidly than nominal GDP, so that the share of health care in GDP rises without limit. If this happened, of course, there would eventually be few or no resources left to produce food, shelter, industrial goods, or education, and the health care burden on households and firms would become intolerable. This cannot happen; therefore, it will not happen. Stein's Law applies: when a trend cannot continue, it will stop.

No understanding of the issues is gained by a procedure that necessarily incorporates unrealistic assumptions of this type. Since the time horizons are arbitrary, the present value of future "liabilities" can be blown up to any size, simply by changing time horizons and discount rates. Most readers of the proposed budgetary documents are unlikely to be aware that the exercise is purely arithmetic in this sense.

WHAT MATTERS: ECONOMIC GROWTH

For Social Security and other permanent programs, what matters for long-range projections are demographics, technology, and economic growth. Financing is virtually irrelevant. If by 2083, everyone is over age 67, no financing scheme will allow us to meet our commitment to let people retire at a decent living standard at age 67. This, however, is most unlikely. Indeed, all plausible projections of demographic trends show only gradual and moderately rising real burdens on those of normal working age in terms of numbers of dependents (aged plus young) per worker. The OASDI (old age, survivors, and disability insurance) part of Social Security currently moves less than 4.5 percent of GDP to beneficiaries and that rises to about 6.5 percent over the next 75 years. On one hand, this is a significant increase, but on the other hand, similar shifts have occurred in the past without generating economic crisis or intolerable burdens. And it still leaves over 93 percent of GDP outside OASDI.

Moreover, the current crisis drives home the necessity of having the Social Security leg of the retirement stool—a leg that promises to deliver benefits no matter how poorly the economy performs. While the promise is in financial terms, because of the manner in which benefits are calculated, benefits will tend to rise in real terms as the economy's capacity to produce rises. As the population ages, there will necessarily be a rise in the real burden of supporting them. The other legs of the retirement stool (private pensions and individual savings) cannot guarantee that the real needs of elders will be met. First, this is because financial markets are subject to wild swings—so that many will retire at inopportune times (when assets are falling in value). Second, there is no mechanism operating in financial markets to ensure that asset values rise sufficiently faster than prices of consumer goods to shift a larger share of the nation's output to the retired. Indeed, it is precisely the ability of Social Security to increase the share of output going to beneficiaries (that is, to raise the real burden) that will be required as the nation ages.

The growing "real burden" of providing for an aging population is captured by the projection that while we have three workers today "supporting" each beneficiary, that will fall to only two workers sometime around mid-century. Two questions follow from this. First, can we expect productivity to rise enough over the next half-century to ensure that two workers will, indeed, produce as much as three today? All reasonable projections—including those of the trustees—do assume this. Indeed, over the past half-century, productivities of workers in manufacturing have doubled or tripled, depending on the industry— far more than what is necessary to guarantee that we will have enough output to raise the living standards of retirees, workers, and other dependents.

Suppose (however unlikely the event) that productivity does not rise by the necessary amount. Is there any *purely* financial change we can make to the program—including privatization—that will avoid a "crisis"? The answer is clearly no. Getting more money into the hands of future retirees would just mean that they'd bid more of tomorrow's production away from workers and other dependents, leaving those groups worse off. To be sure, there would be policy actions that could attenuate the crisis by raising the ratio of workers to retirees (immigration in 2050 of workers, for example)—but financial expedients are not among them.

In short, it serves no useful purpose to project financial shortfalls for Social Security and Medicare into a far distant future, and no purpose whatever to revise those programs today on the basis of such projections. The notion that there is some "unfunded liability" amounting to tens of trillions of dollars is hogwash. The U.S. government always has the operational ability to make all payments as they come due, and could do so even if through some strange accounting mistake or trick one concluded that government liabilities exceed private assets.

MY STORY about Social Security begins near the shoreline of Lake Erie on a quiet street in Point Place, Ohio. Here, in the mid-1960s, Peter, my husband, and I had chosen to raise our children. The community abutted the Michigan State line and bustled with similar young families who'd purchased their first tract houses. The close, friendly neighborhood spanned three short streets.

Six-year-old Danny was looking forward to first grade in the fall. Diane, a rambunctious four-year-old with red hair, and chubby seven-month-old Paul completed our family.

On a late June evening, our friend Richard joined us for dinner. He arrived on his Harley. My husband's eyes lit up when he saw the bike, almost a replica of one he'd owned when he was in the Air Force. Supper ended and Peter borrowed the motorcycle to complete his church canvassing.

I'd gone inside to bathe baby Paul while Richard played with the other children. Mid-bath, the phone rang and that moment changed our lives forever. An accident had left my husband seriously injured.

All week Peter lay in a coma, fighting for his life. On the eighth day, he died.

I'd been a stay-at-home Mom and now I was a twenty-seven-year-old widow with three small children. A horrifying grief gripped my heart leaving me numb—powerless. Then slowly, another pain and an inner panic began to take hold. How could I manage funeral expenses, medical bills, a mortgage, and three children to feed and clothe? Our small insurance policy was inadequate.

My working mother—a widow living on the West Coast—came to help. She insisted I set an appointment with the Social Security Administration and apply for spousal and dependent benefits. She helped me complete the paperwork and I was eligible.

The benefits provided economic security for me and my children. It also gave me the chance to reinvent my life. I was able to heal and prepare for our future.

All three children grew and thrived to become productive, successful adults. I shudder to think what would have happened to the four of us without Social Security benefits.

I will be forever grateful to our Social Security system.

— SANDRA STARK —
VANCOUVER, WASHINGTON

One America, Linked by the Dignity of Each and the Destiny of All

BARACK OBAMA

In this speech delivered at the National Press Club in Washington in April 26, 2005, for the Franklin and Eleanor Roosevelt Institute to celebrate the 70th anniversary of Social Security, a newly elected senator from Illinois makes an eloquent case for rejecting the efforts of the Bush Administration to privatize Social Security. He says, "You know, there are times in the life of this nation where we are individual citizens, going about our business, enjoying the freedoms that we've been blessed with. And then there are times when we're one America, linked by the dignity of each and the destiny of all. Debate over the future of Social Security needs to be one of those latter times." Senator [now President] Obama knows first-hand the importance of Social Security; he spent many of his childhood years with his grandparents, for whom Social Security provided an important portion of their income. During the presidential campaign, he said of his grandmother (who passed away two days before he was elected president), "She was able to have a secure retirement because of Social Security and because of a pension through her job. . . . Knowing she is secure is so important to me."

*B*y the time the Senate Finance Committee holds the first Senate hearing on President Bush's Social Security plan today, we'll have heard just about everything there is to be said about the issue.

We'll have heard about privatization, about benefit cuts, wage indexing, lifting caps. We will have been scared into thinking that the system will go broke when our kids retire, despite some evidence to the contrary.

I am going to be happy to address all these particular issues during the question-and-answer period of my talk here today. But like Jim [James Roosevelt, Jr. introduced Senator Obama], rather than focus simply on the usual back and forth of the debate, one of the things I want to do today is to think about some of the larger issues that are at stake in the Social Security debate that's taking place in this country.

I can't help thinking about the America that FDR saw when he looked out from the window of the White House from his wheelchair: an America where too many were ill-fed, ill-clothed, ill-housed, and insecure; an America where more and more Americans were finding themselves on the losing end of the new economy and where there was nothing available to cushion their fall.

Some thought that our country didn't have a responsibility to do anything about these problems, that people would be better off left to their own devices and the whims of the market.

Others believed that American capitalism had failed and that it was time to try something else altogether.

But our President, FDR, believed deeply in the American idea. He understood that the freedom to pursue our own individual dreams is made possible by the promise that if fate causes us to stumble or fall, our larger American family will be there to lift us up; that if we're willing to share even a small amount of life's risks and rewards with each other, then we'll all have a chance to achieve our God-given potential.

And because Franklin Roosevelt had the courage to act on this idea, individual Americans were able to get back on their feet and build an unprecedented shared prosperity that's still the envy of the world.

The New Deal gave laid-off workers a guarantee that he or she could count on unemployment insurance to put food on the table while they looked for a new job.

It gave the young man who suffered a debilitating accident assurance that he could count on disability benefits to get him through the tough times.

A widow might still be able to raise her children despite the loss of a spouse without the indignity of asking for charity.

And Franklin Roosevelt's greatest legacy promised the couple who put in a lifetime of sacrifice and hard work that they could retire with dignity and respect because of Social Security.

Today, we're told by those who want to privatize, that how much things have changed since FDR's days justifies the proposals that they're making.

I couldn't agree more that things have changed drastically since FDR's time. A child born in this new century is likely to start his life with both parents or a single parent working full-time jobs. They'll try their hardest to juggle work and family but they'll end up needing child care to keep that child safe, cared for, and educated.

They'll want to give him the best education possible. But unless they live in a wealthy town with good public schools, they'll have to settle for less or find the money for private schools.

That student, as he or she gets older, will study hard and dream of going to the best colleges in America. But with tuition rising higher and faster than ever before, 519 percent over the last 25 years, he or she may have to postpone those dreams or start life deeper in debt than any generation before them.

And when that student graduates from college, he or she will find a job market where middle-class manufacturing jobs with good benefits have long been replaced with low-wage, low-benefit service sector jobs and high-skill, high-wage jobs of the future.

To get those good jobs, this young man or young woman will need the skills and knowledge not only to compete with other workers in America, but with highly skilled and knowledgeable workers from all over the world who are being recruited by the same companies that once made their home in the United States of America.

And when this student, he or she, finally starts a job, he'll want health insurance. But rising costs mean that fewer employers can afford to provide the benefits. And when they do, fewer employees can afford the premiums, the co-payments, and the deductibles.

When this young man or young woman starts a family, he or she will want to buy a house and a car and pay for child care and college for his or her own children. But as he or she watches the lucky few benefit from lucrative bonuses and tax shelters, he'll see that his own tax burden, when you combine the federal, state, and local, is rising and his own paycheck is barely [sufficient to cover] this month's bills.

And when he retires, he'll hope that he and his wife have saved enough. But if there wasn't enough to save for retirement, he'll hope that there will still be at least two Social Security checks that come to the house every month.

Here's the point: There are challenges that we are facing in the twenty-first century that we shouldn't exaggerate. We're not seeing the absolute deprivations of the Great Depression. But it cannot be denied that families face more risk and greater insecurity than we have known for a very long time, even as those families have fewer resources available to pull themselves out of difficult situations.

Whereas people once were able to count on their employers to provide health care, pensions and a job that would last a lifetime, today's workers wonder if suffering a heart attack will cause his employer to drop his coverage. He has to worry about how much he can contribute to his own pension fund. And he fears the possibility that he might walk into work tomorrow and find his job outsourced.

Now, just as the naysayers in Roosevelt's day told us that there was nothing we could do to help people help themselves, people in power today are telling us that instead of sharing the risks of this new economy, we should make them shoulder those risks on their own.

In the end, that's what I think the debate over the future of Social Security is all about. After a lifetime of hard work and contribution to this country, do we tell our seniors that they're on their own? Or do we tell them that we're here to help make sure that they have a basic decent standard of living?

Is the dignity of life in their latter years their problem or one we all share?

Since this is Washington, you won't hear some of these questions answered directly. Instead, what you'll hear is talk of reform. Although what's actually meant is privatization.

You'll hear talk of strengthening which is actually a euphemism for dismantling.

(*LAUGHTER*)

They will tell us that there's a crisis to get us all riled up, to sit down and listen to their plan to privatize but there's not going to be much discussion about some alternatives that would actually shore up the system.

Here's what we know: Under the President's proposal to privatize,

191

we are looking at cutting guaranteed benefits by at least 40 and up to 50 percent.

We know that the transition costs involved in shifting to a new system would involve borrowing between $2 trillion and $5 trillion from countries like China and Japan.

We know, of course, that fiscal conservatives hate debt and deficit, so we haven't had too much discussion about the specifics of how that would be paid for.

(*LAUGHTER*)

And it's not even about the ability of private accounts to finance the gap on the system. We know that. Even the proponents of privatization have stated that this will not solve the very real funding gap that we'll be experiencing in 35 or 40 years.

So what is this whole thing about? And why have some in power been pushing so hard for so long now? It's probably summed up in one sentence in one White House memo that somehow made its way out of the White House. And I give credit to the White House: this doesn't happen very often.

(*LAUGHTER*)

The memo reads: "For the first time in six decades the Social Security battle is one we can win. And in doing so, we can help transform the political and philosophical landscape of the country."

There it is. Since Social Security was first signed into law, almost 70 years ago, by James [Roosevelt]'s grandfather, at a time when FDR's opponents were calling it a hoax that would never work and that some likened to Communism, there has been movement, there has been movement after movement to get rid of the program for purely ideological reasons.

Because some still believe that we can't solve the problems we face as one American community, they think this country works better when we're left to face fate by ourselves.

And I understand this view. I understand this perspective. There is something bracing about the Social Darwinist idea: the idea that there isn't a problem that the unfettered free market cannot solve. It requires no sacrifice on the part of those of us who've won life's lottery.

It doesn't require us to consider how lucky we are to have the parents we did or the education that we received or the right breaks at the right time.

But I fundamentally disagree with the central premise of what this President has termed the ownership society. And that's what I significantly object to when it comes to the current privatization of Social Security.

What is it exactly that we're going to be telling retirees whose investments in the stock markets have gone badly: that we're sorry; keep working; you're on your own?

When people's expected benefits get cut and they have to choose between groceries and their prescriptions, what will we say then; that's not our problem?

When our debt climbs so high that our children face sky-high taxes, just as they are starting their first job, what are we going to tell them; deal with it?

This isn't how America works. This isn't how we saved millions of seniors from a life of poverty 70 years ago. This isn't how we sent the greatest generation of veterans to college so they could build the greatest middle class in American history. And this isn't how we should face the challenges of the future either.

And yet this is the direction that we are trying to take America in, that those in power are trying to take America in, in every aspect of public policy.

Instead of trying to contain skyrocketing costs of health care and expand access to the uninsured, we have the health savings account, which basically means that we're going to leave the system alone, eliminate employer-based health care, give you $5,000, and you deal with 15 percent inflation every year.

And I don't know how you deal with it. Well, maybe you just go to the doctor less. That's the idea behind the consumer-driven health care reform model: You go to the doctor less, or you have your child go to the doctor less.

Instead of strengthening a pension system that provides defined benefits to employees who have worked a lifetime, we'll give you a modest tax break. Of course, we'll give you a larger tax break the more money you make and hope that you invest well and save well in your own little account.

And if none of this works, if you can't find affordable insurance or you suffer an illness that leaves you thousands of dollars in debt, then you should no longer count on being able to start over, because we've changed the bankruptcy laws to make sure that the burden of the debt is squarely on your shoulders.

Taking responsibility for one's self, showing individual initiative: these are American values that we all share. Frankly, they are values that we could stand to see more of in a culture where the buck is all too often passed to the next guy. Those are values, by the way, that we could see more of and use more of here in Washington.

But the irony of this all-out assault against every existing form of social insurance is that these safety nets are exactly what encourages each of us to be risk takers, what encourages entrepreneurship, what allows us to pursue our individual ambitions. It happens at the smallest scale and at the largest scale.

We get into our cars knowing that if someone rear-ends us, we'll have insurance to pay for the repairs. We buy a house knowing that our investment is protected by homeowner's insurance. We take a chance on start-ups and small businesses, because we know if they fail, there are protections available to cushion our fall.

Corporations obtain limited liability, precisely because we understand that the free market works when people know that utter destitution is not going to be their destination in case their venture fails.

And it's that same reason why we need social insurance to provide people some confidence that in fact as they move around freely pursuing their dreams, pursuing their ambitions, pursuing a vision of what might be accomplished, that they know that they're not in it alone each and every time.

That's how America works. And if we want to keep it working, we need to develop new ways for all of us to share the new risks of a twenty-first-century economy, not destroy those that we already have.

The genius of Roosevelt was putting into practice the idea that America doesn't have to be a place where individual aspirations are at war with our common good; it's a place where one makes the other possible.

Now, I think we will save Social Security from privatization this year. And in doing so, I think we will affirm our belief that we are all connected as one people, ready to share life's risks and rewards for the benefit of each and the good of all.

Let me close by suggesting that the Democrats are absolutely united in the need to strengthen Social Security and make it solvent for future generations. We know that, and we want that. And I believe that both Democrats and Republicans can work together to accomplish that.

And while we're at it, we can begin a debate about the real challenges America faces as baby boomers begin to retire: about getting a handle on ever-spiraling health care costs; about increasing individual and national savings; about strengthening our pension system for the twenty-first century.

These are all important questions that require us to work together, not in a manufactured panic, but in a genuine spirit of solving problems with pragmatism and innovation that will offer every American the secure retirement that they have earned.

You know, there are times in the life of this nation where we are individual citizens, going about our business, enjoying the freedoms that we've been blessed with.

And then there are times when we're one America, linked by the dignity of each and the destiny of all

Debate over the future of Social Security needs to be one of those latter times.

I have had 19 town hall meetings in Illinois since I was elected. And the people I've met have told me they don't want big government running their lives, but they do want an active government that will give them the opportunity to make the most of their lives. Starting with the child born today and the senior moving into the twilight of life, together I think we can provide that opportunity.

The day that Franklin Delano Roosevelt signed the Social Security Act of 1935, he began by saying, "Today, a hope of many years standing is in large part fulfilled."

It's now time to fulfill our hope for an America where we're in this together, for our seniors, for our children, and for every American in the years and generations yet to come.

Thank you very much.

(*APPLAUSE*)

I FIRST FOUND out about Social Security benefits in October of 1995, when my husband passed away in a fatal car accident that we were in. It also left my 4-month-old son disabled for life. At that time I was 20 years old, not working, and having to care for a baby who needed a lot of medical care. If it wasn't for Social Security survivors benefits, I don't think I could care for my child the way I did. Social Security gave me the opportunity to stay at home with my child and take him to therapy and to provide the best care that I could offer. Once my son went to a special day school, I also was able to go back to school and get a degree. Since he is permanently disabled, Social Security will provide him with benefits that will help him be independent and have a good quality life regardless of his disability.

— MARIZA HERNANDEZ —
ONTARIO, CALIFORNIA

The Mythology of Fear

James Roosevelt, Jr.

James Roosevelt, Jr., is president and chief executive officer of Tufts Health Plan, a non-profit health insurance plan that serves 736,000 members in Massachusetts and Rhode Island. He was previously associate commissioner for Retirement Policy for the Social Security Administration in Washington, D.C. He served as part of the transition team for President Barack Obama by co-chairing a review of the Social Security Administration. His grandfather, Franklin Delano Roosevelt, gave his fellow citizens a secure life foundation when he signed Social Security into law in August 1935. Today 54 million Americans receive Social Security.

The essay below is the text of the keynote speech James Roosevelt delivered at the National Press Club in Washington on August 6, 2010, to the annual Retirement Research Conference in commemoration of the 75th Anniversary of Social Security.

$\mathcal{A}$lmost 75 years ago to the day, President Franklin Delano Roosevelt, spoke these words:

> We can never insure one-hundred percent of the population against one-hundred percent of the hazards and vicissitudes of life. But we have tried to frame a law which will give some measure of protection to the average citizen and to his family against . . . poverty-ridden old age. This law, too, represents a cornerstone in a structure, which is being built, but is by no means complete. . . . It is . . . a law that will take care of human needs and at the same time provide for the United States an economic structure of vastly greater soundness.

My grandfather uttered these words on August 14, 1935, on the proud occasion of his signing the Social Security Act into law. They expressed a fundamental belief shared by him and my grandmother that all people should be free from fear of want and destitution. My grandparents possessed an almost boundless sense of optimism in the American people; freed from our fears, they had faith that we could move mountains. Thus, in 1933, President Roosevelt summoned the courage of the American people with the immortal words: "the only thing we have to fear is fear itself."

I am deeply honored to have this opportunity to share my thoughts with you on the occasion of the 75th anniversary of Social Security. My grandfather left many legacies. The history of the second half of the twentieth century would have been much darker save for the light he shone. Social Security is one of those legacies, one that has both transformed American society while also reflecting its most enduring values.

While this is an occasion for celebration, I am also deeply troubled. I am deeply troubled by the torrent of distortions, deceptions, and falsehoods being unleashed by the enemies of Social Security. Their strategy is as simple as it is reprehensible: sow enough concern and fear about the program—fears that Social Security is not working, is bankrupting the country, and cannot be counted on in the future—and you can convince people of the need for radical solutions.

While there are currently no frontal assaults on Social Security akin to what President George W. Bush unleashed in 2005, there are more insidious dangers. There are ominous signs that the National Commission on Fiscal Responsibility and Reform (better known as the Deficit Commission) has set its sights on Social Security. It is deeply disturbing that the co-chairman of that commission, former Senator Alan Simpson, has been using this platform to put forward the same baseless claims about the program: that it's "insolvent, it's paying out more than it's taking in" or "there is no surplus in there," "there" being the Social Security Trust Fund.

Fear, my grandfather said, is "nameless, unreasoning, unjustified terror which paralyzes needed efforts to convert retreat into advance." I believe that if we hold the distortions, deceptions, and falsehoods up to the light of truth, we can convert retreat into advance. The truth about Social Security is that it has contributed to the financial well-being of almost every American family; it is completely solvent today because it has a dedicated income stream that covers its costs and is actuarially sound; it will remain solvent for decades to come with only minor adjustments; and it has consistently run a surplus and should be "off the table" in the deficit commission's deliberations. As Nancy Altman wrote in her book, *The Battle for Social Security*, "Armed with the proper insight and understanding, we Americans can assert our will and demand that the program envisioned by Franklin Roosevelt remain his enduring legacy."

SOCIAL SECURITY HAS TRANSFORMED AMERICAN SOCIETY

Social Security has been the most successful government program of the past 75 years. No program has touched more American lives and benefitted more American families. Today, approximately 52 million Americans receive Social Security benefits each month. Even those who have not drawn a single Social Security check have benefitted. While it was forged in the heat of the Depression, Social Security remains every bit as relevant and important to Americans today. With only minor adjustments, this program will be there for Americans who have not yet been born.

The success of the program is rooted in the two words that comprise its name: "social" and "security." Social Security is a *social* insurance program for American families. It is rooted in our belief that as members of society we have obligations to each other. We are committed to protecting our fellow Americans from the economic ravages of old age, disability, and death. We see a benefit in spreading risks across society rather than placing the full burden of what my grandfather called the "hazards and vicissitudes of life" on individuals and individual families. These obligations extend across time. One generation supports the next generation, which supports the next generation and so on.

As Barack Obama stated in his very first speech before the National Press Club, which he delivered in 2005 on the topic of Social Security, "we are all connected as one people—ready to share life's risks and rewards for the benefit of each and good of all."

This social dimension is what the libertarian critics of Social Security fail to grasp. Their individualistic, atomistic conception of society doesn't allow for the generosity of spirit and the deep connections Americans feel for their fellow citizens.

The "security" in Social Security is vitally important to Americans. My grandfather thought of Social Security as part of a three-legged stool of financial security. Social Security would provide an income floor below which no American family would fall as a result of old age, disability, or death. Social Security was not intended to stand alone; it was to be supplemented by savings and private pension systems. Today, it may be more accurate to think of Social Security as the bedrock of a secure retirement, as the two other legs in the stool have become increasingly wobbly. Private pension plans are looking more and more like historical anomalies, as they currently cover only about 20 percent of private sector employees. And the national savings rate, despite its current positive blip, provides little comfort that contemporary Americans are any better able to provide for their later years than our forebears.

Americans understand that "there but for the grace of God go I." They want to protect their families from the tragedies that can befall anyone and which no one can control. The pushers of ill-conceived privatization schemes miss the point that Americans want to be able to count on something real for themselves and their families. They might be willing to assume greater risks in their 401(k) accounts to earn higher returns, but this is because they have Social Security on which to fall back.

Economists are finding that low probability events, like stock market crashes, occur much more frequently than we think. Or as economists would put it, the "thin tails" of a normal distribution curve are often fatter than we suspect. Stock markets have experienced two "once in a generation" declines in just the past 10 years. Then think of how many employees saw their nest eggs destroyed by the corruption of their bosses at Enron and the like. From the perspective of individuals who are retired or hope to retire soon, these were catastrophic events that significantly lowered their expected standard of living. But there stands Social Security. Beneficiaries can mark their calendars by the arrival of their check each month.

Social Security has truly transformed American society. In 1959, 35 percent of Americans aged 65 and older had family incomes below the federal poverty line. Today that figure is 10 percent—marking more than a 70 percent reduction in the proportion of elderly Americans living in poverty. In my grandparents' day, old age was something to be feared. Today, despite financial challenges such as the high costs of prescription drugs, Social Security provides retirees with much greater financial security and peace of mind. If we took away Social Security benefits, it is estimated that nearly half of elderly people would have incomes below the poverty line.

It is interesting that many critics of Social Security make an "intergenerational equity" argument that the program is not fair to workers paying into the system today. Of course, most of this argument depends on the utterly baseless assumption that Social Security will not pay future retirement benefits to people contributing today. But let's even assume for one minute that that were true. Think about the burdens that young families would face today if they also had to provide financial support or a home for their aging parents. Think about the extreme hardships many families would endure if not for the long-term disability and survivor benefits that Social Security provides. We associate Social Security with retirees but nearly one in five recipients of Social Security benefits are children under the age of 18. They may be children whose father is disabled or whose mother was killed in the attacks on 9/11. Families face many financial stresses, from the costs of food to health care to college, but there are many stresses that they don't have to bear because of Social Security. The essentials of providing clothing and shelter are stresses that are lessened for people receiving Social Security.

It is not surprising then that Social Security is so popular with the American people. Poll after poll confirms this. The enemies of Social Security have gotten the message. For the most part, they no longer talk about eliminating or privatizing Social Security. Instead they speak in Orwellian language about "saving," "strengthening," and "protecting" Social Security. To advance their hidden radical agenda, they have developed a "mythology of fear," trotting out their themes of a program that is "in crisis," "bankrupt," "broke," and, in the wake of Madoff, even a "ponzi scheme."

Sharron Angle, the darling of the Tea Party and the Republican Party nominee in the Nevada Senate race, has repeatedly called for phasing out Social Security over time, characterizing it as "a broken system without much to recommend it." She has voiced support for shifting younger workers to private retirement accounts, an idea similar to what former President George W. Bush proposed six years ago in his veiled effort to dismantle the program. Now the handlers have gotten to her. Suddenly she is saying that "I want to save Medicare and Social Security." Well, I, for one, am glad that she has seen the light. But I don't think my idea of saving Social Security and hers are probably aligned. In fact, Social Security does not need to be *saved*, at all.

Most Americans can see through the deception, but I am wary that many Americans, as much as they support Social Security, are questioning whether it will be there when they retire. This is a dangerous trend. Social Security needs to do more to educate Americans of the benefits and stability of Social Security. We need to debunk those "nameless, unreasoning, unjustified terrors" that are being perpetuated by those whose philosophy of economics doesn't take into account the unarguable success of Social Security.

SOCIAL SECURITY IS FINANCIALLY STABLE

There is a saying that if you repeat something often enough it becomes the truth. Nothing better illustrates that point than the notion that Social Security will be bankrupted by baby boomers. Supposedly it is the enormous bulge of retirees from this generation that will sink Social Security once and for all. Indeed, the generation of Americans born between 1946 and 1964, who drew their first retirement checks from Social Security in 2008, will place heavy demands upon the system as they reach their retirement years. But this is also a generation that has been paying into the system since they started working in the early 1960s. The critics of Social Security often "forget"—conveniently I think—about the "pay it forward" aspect of Social Security. They "forget" that Social Security is an insurance program, where people need to contribute before they collect. The baby boomers have been contributing to Social Security for more than 40 years. It is their contributions that have built the massive surpluses that Social Security has amassed. Much of the money that the baby boomers are and will be drawing from Social Security is and will be their own.

We have known about the impact of the baby boom generation for a long time. It isn't as if we woke up yesterday and discovered that there are millions of new retirees about to draw on Social Security. The last of the baby boomers was born in 1964.

And we have been planning for the impact of this generation on Social Security for a long time. Congress has enacted ten significant Social Security bills in the last 60 years. As Nancy Altman has pointed out, "every enactment has taken into account the baby boom, and each has left the program in long-run actuarial balance."

In fact, the projected deficit of Social Security beginning in 2037 is really not a result of the baby boomers. Forward-thinking Social Security Administration actuaries had already accounted for them. Instead, changes in the projected deficit have more to do with factors such as economic and wage growth, productivity, and disability rates.

But these important parts of the story are usually left out. Instead the purveyors of fear want you to believe that the baby boomers are retiring on the backs of their children and grandchildren. If you buy this premise, then they pull out their frightening statistics showing a declining number of contributors supporting a rising number of beneficiaries of Social Security to "prove" that the program is unsustainable.

These utter distortions, however, are nothing new. My grandfather had to contend with them. In the 1936 presidential campaign, the Republican nominee, Alf Landon, labeled Social Security a "hoax." In dismissing Social Security as "unworkable," the GOP platform of that year stated that Social Security would be unable to pay benefits to two-thirds of retirees. My grandfather then would not be surprised by the fear mongering of today. Indeed, Social Security's critics have been casting the same aspersions on the program for 75 years.

In the 1964 presidential campaign, Barry Goldwater asserted that Social Security "promises more benefits to more people than the incomes collected will provide." During the same election, Ronald Reagan, campaigning on behalf of Mr. Goldwater, warned of Social Security's "fiscal shortcomings" and derided it as a "welfare program." In 1980, the libertarian Cato Institute predicted that Social Security would go bankrupt by 2006. In the 2000 campaign, presidential candidate George W. Bush warned that "it's going to be impossible to bridge the gap without causing huge payroll taxes or major benefit reductions."

The interesting thing about all of these dire warnings of Social Security's demise is just how exaggerated they have been. Prognosticators of Social Security's impending doom are the political equivalent of weathermen: the storms often peter out or don't turn out to be nearly as severe as they predicted. The difference, however, is that weathermen get most of their forecasts right and generally don't play fast and loose with the facts. Despite the prognosticators' poor track record, the mythology of fear surrounding Social Security has seeped into our collective conscience. Polls suggest that a majority of Americans don't expect to receive Social Security benefits when they retire.

Now let's take a true measure of where we are. Social Security has not only been the most effective government program, it has been the most responsible government program. Social Security costs are funded out of its own dedicated revenue stream. It does not and cannot borrow money to finance its operations. There is no deficit financing. Social Security is the epitome of Yankee frugality. It could not be better managed. Social Security returns more than 99 cents to beneficiaries on every dollar collected. I dare you to find a private retirement plan that can claim that.

By the end of calendar year 2009, the Social Security Trust Fund had a *positive* balance of $2.54 trillion. Let me repeat: a 2.54 *trillion dollar surplus*. It is estimated that Social Security revenues (including interest on the Trust Fund) will continue to exceed expenditures through 2024. As a result of interest earned on the Trust Fund balances, the Trust Fund surplus will continue to expand to approximately $4.3 trillion in 2023. After that year, it is projected that the balance in the Social Security Trust Fund will begin to decline. Still, reserves will be sufficient to pay full benefits through the year 2037. After 2037, Social Security would still be able to pay for 78 percent of benefits.

Now since when is news that a program is completely solvent for 27 years bad news? Even in year 28 and thereafter it could still fund three-quarters of anticipated benefits. This is decidedly NOT a program that's broke, going broke, or won't be there when current contributors retire. In fact this is quite a remarkable achievement.

I think if Americans really understood its true financial picture, those poll numbers suggesting people are not counting on Social Security would be reversed. Doubt would give way to confidence, fear to security.

When Social Security celebrates its 100th anniversary (and I accept your invitation to speak before you in August 2035 on the occasion of your 37th Annual Conference), it will still have money in the bank. That's assuming we do absolutely nothing to make it even more secure.

Why assume that we will stand still? As the May 2010 report of the Senate Special Committee on Aging concluded, there are any number of *small, incremental measures* that would keep Social Security solvent for the next *75 years*. I won't commit now to speaking before you in 2085, but I am confident you will find someone who will be as equally honored as I am to speak before you about the success and stability of Social Security.

The point is we don't have to make radical changes to the program to keep it working for future generations of Americans. That would be like overhauling a car engine when all we need to do is change the oil. We don't need to scrap a secure program of social insurance for a risky individual self-help scheme, as the slick salesmen of privatization keep trying to convince us.

What are the policy equivalents of oil changes that will keep the program running? The Senate Special Committee on Aging has considered a range of options, which alone or in combination can keep Social Security completely solvent almost into the next century. For example, increasing employee and employer contribution rates by 1.1 percent—from the current 6.2 percent to 7.3 percent—would eliminate the *entire* projected shortfall (i.e., provide 100 percent of benefits after the year 2037 through 2085).

We could eliminate the cap on wages subject to Social Security contributions. In 2010, only earnings up to $106,800 are subject to FICA. In creating the cap, Congress intended to cover 90 percent of the aggregate wages of all workers. Today, because wages have been increasing faster than the cap—especially for the top 5 percent of wage earners—FICA is assessed on only 83 percent of aggregate wages. If we eliminated the cap, even if we counted all the increased earnings toward benefits, we would eliminate an estimated 95 percent of the shortfall. And this change would impact only the top 6 percent of wage earners in this country.

We might also consider expanding the base of workers covered by Social Security. Almost all workers pay into the system, with the exception of about one-quarter of state and municipal government employees who are covered by alternative pension systems. In my home state of Massachusetts, for instance, almost 95 percent of state and local government workers do not pay into Social Security. If we extended Social Security to all newly hired state and local employees over the next five years, the Special Committee on Aging estimates we would eliminate almost 10 percent of the projected deficit, while also eliminating another burden on state and local governments.

Former Social Security Commissioner Robert Ball—whose reasoned voice is one I dearly miss—and Nancy Altman have developed a plan that would keep Social Security running for at least another three-quarters of a century without cutting any benefits and not increasing the FICA rate for approximately 19 out of 20 American workers. Their plan would gradually raise the cap to cover 90 percent of aggregate wages, as Congress intended. Again, this change would affect only a small proportion of the American public, and if phased in over the next 20 to 30 years, would have no discernible financial impact on them. Second, Ball-Altman would restore a residual estate tax at 2009 levels and dedicate those revenues to the Social Security system. The estate tax would affect only individuals with estates of more than $3.5 million. Finally, they would allow Social Security gradually to invest some of its Trust Fund assets into equities to earn somewhat higher returns, just as other public and private pension plans do. While the private equity markets pose higher risks, the risk will not be borne by individuals (as in the privatization schemes). Since Social Security will be around for quite some time, the risks are mitigated by being spread over many more years.

I am not here to advocate for one solution or the other. What I am here to say is that there are many smart people who have figured out how we can make modest changes to Social Security that will keep benefits flowing to millions of American families for decades to come.

There are some ideas that I wholeheartedly oppose. First, I am absolutely against any cut in payment levels. Social Security pays only modest amounts to begin with. The average benefit check is around $1,100. Cutting benefits would expose millions of Americans to financial distress—especially the one-third of elderly retirees who depend on Social Security for 90 percent or more of their income.

We should not contemplate raising the retirement age at which workers can collect benefits, as many are proposing, unless we revamp the disability system under Social Security. Any change must account for occupational differences and requires more nuanced, analytical judgments about which people can reasonably be expected to work to a later age before collecting. Without revamping the disability system to improve its efficiency as well as its scope, raising the eligibility age could create unacceptable hardship for whole groups of workers. Any reform must meet the twin demands of fiscal savings and equity.

The United States does not have a Social Security crisis. It never did. What we do have is fear of a crisis. It is fear that has been fed by the propagation and accumulation of myths about the program. If we let our fears rule our judgment we will undo the greatest government program in our history, one that has eliminated poverty for millions of Americans and supported millions of families in time of need.

KEEP SOCIAL SECURITY OFF THE TABLE

This brings us to the current National Commission on Fiscal Responsibility and Reform. While I am deeply supportive of President Obama's efforts to control the burgeoning federal budget deficit, I am deeply concerned that he has instructed the commission that "everything has to be on the table," including Social Security.

It's not that I think Social Security is "sacred" compared to other worthy government programs, although I have a rather personal stake in its continuance. It doesn't belong on the table because it's *different* from other programs. By law, the receipts and disbursements of Social Security Trust Funds are excluded from the President's budget and the budget resolution passed by Congress. Social Security has its own revenue source, is prohibited from borrowing funds or going into debt, and can only pay benefits from its own funds. Social Security should be out of reach of the Budget Deficit Commission because it is not part of the federal budget.

Since Social Security has not contributed in any way to the deficit, it makes no sense to consider it as part of the solution.

I am afraid that by placing Social Security under the purview of the deficit commission we are contributing to the mythology of fear around Social Security. That mythology says the program is heading for bankruptcy and is unsustainable. That mythology says the program will not be there for our children and our children's children.

I am concerned that although Social Security contributes nothing to the deficit, it will be targeted by its enemies on the commission. Its enemies have failed in their frontal assaults on Social Security but now they have been given cover by a deficit commission. The opponents of Social Security have been biding their time waiting for an opportunity to attack Social Security without being seen as attacking it. The deficit commission is that opportunity. "We love Social Security but we can't afford it" will be their new battle cry.

The recent tirade by deficit commission cochair Alan Simpson only confirms my suspicions, lest anyone think I am being overly alarmist. Facts have not gotten in the way of Simpson's determination to target Social Security. Let's examine some of the false statements he made about Social Security.

Alan Simpson says Social Security "will go broke in 2037."

The reality is that Social Security will be able to pay 76 percent of benefits after 2037, even if we do nothing to adjust it.

Alan Simpson says "There's no surplus in there. It's just a bunch of IOUs."

The reality is those IOUs are U.S. Treasury bonds, which have the backing of the full faith and credit of the U.S. government. Investors all over the world invest in U.S. Treasury bonds. There simply is no more secure asset on the face of the planet. But Mr. Simpson would have individuals invest their hard-earned money in the stock market. In the long run the stock market may be a good investment. But in the short run, the value of an individual's private retirement account can change dramatically. I for one am glad that I'm not retiring anytime soon, given the battering my 401(k) has taken in the past few years. Further evidence of the prudence of the Social Security system is found in the legal requirement that the Treasury pay interest on bonds held by Social Security that is equal to the highest rate it pays on any bonds at the time of their issue.

Mr. Simpson would also have us believe that "There is more going out than coming in" to the Social Security Trust Fund. Again the reality is that the Trust Fund has a surplus of $2.4 trillion dollars. That surplus is projected to continue to grow for the next 13 years, despite all those baby boomers starting to receive monthly checks.

As Paul Krugman recently pointed out on his blog, the deficit hawks want to have it both ways when it comes to Social Security. They want to treat Social Security as just another program in the federal budget, so they don't need to credit it for the quarter century and billions of dollars worth of surpluses it has accumulated (surpluses which of course are denominated in those worthless IOUs anyway). But they want to view Social Security as a program unto itself when the time comes that its payments exceed its annual revenues (which we said before is projected to occur in 2016), so they can claim it is going broke. It is completely nonsensical and deceitful to try to have it both ways.

IT IS TIME TO STOP PLAYING POLITICS WITH SOCIAL SECURITY

It is time to stop playing politics with the retirements of American workers. It is time to stop playing politics with the disability benefits millions of children and families rely on.

That's where you come in. Sound information is the best antidote to the mythology of fear. Discussions about the future of Social Security should and need to happen, but those conversations must be based on facts and not sweeping and often inaccurate generalizations. You must be nimble in producing data to counter the unreasonable and inflammatory remarks of those who would destroy Social Security. You need to speak out through carefully researched reports and publications in professional journals. But it's also vital to reach a wider public through op-eds, letters to the editor, and testimony. We have to expose the distortions, deceptions, and falsehoods up to the light of truth. We have to restore the faith of each American in the promise of Social Security.

That promise is one that every president since my grandfather has made a solemn vow to protect. President Ford said, "We must begin by insuring that the Social Security system is beyond challenge. [It is] a vital obligation each generation has to those who have worked hard and contributed to it all their lives." Even President Reagan, speaking on the occasion of the signing of the 1983 Social Security Amendments, stated, "[This law] assures the elderly that America will always keep the promises made in troubled times a half century ago. . . . " And President George H.W. Bush affirmed, "To every American out there on Social Security, to every American supporting that system today, and to everyone counting on it when they retire, we made a promise to you, and we are going to keep it."

Democrats and Republicans alike have supported the Social Security system. They have done so because Social Security is rooted in fundamental American values. It is rooted in our belief in individual responsibility. As President Truman noted, "Social Security . . . is not a dole or a device for giving everybody something for nothing. True Social Security must consist of rights which are earned rights—guaranteed by the law of the land." And it is rooted in the obligations we have to each other as Americans. It is rooted, as President Clinton remarked, in "the duties we owe to our parents, the duties we owe to each other when we're differently situated in life, the duties we owe to our children and our grandchildren. Indeed, it reflects our determination to move forward . . . as one America."

My grandfather led this nation through some of its darkest moments, the Great Depression and World War II—periods in our history when the characteristic courage of Americans was most tested. He called on us to rise above our fears. America answered his call.

His generation and the generations that followed have built the most prosperous, the most powerful, and the most generous nation in human history.

Social Security embodies my grandfather's determination to free us from fear by securing the American people against some of the "hazards and vicissitudes of life." It would be tragic if that "nameless, unreasoning, unjustified terror which paralyzes needed efforts to convert retreat into advance" was manipulated to destroy his greatest legacy.

Endnotes

Introduction by Christopher Breiseth

1   Students at the Telluride House subsequently invited Frances Perkins to live with them, which she did from the fall of 1960 until her death in May of 1965. For an account of her life in Telluride House, see Christopher N. Breiseth, "The Frances Perkins I Knew," written in 1966: http://www.fdrheritage.org/breiseth_on_perkins.pdf.

America Before Social Security by Adam Cohen

1   Robin Toner, "Life Before Social Security," *The New York Times*, Jan. 23, 2005; "Pre Social Security Period," http://www.ssa.gov/history/briefhistory3.html
2   Frances Perkins, *The Roosevelt I Knew*, New York: Viking Press, 1946, p. 187.
3   Nancy J. Altman, "Social Security and the Low-Income Worker," 56 American University Law Review 1139, 1142.
4   "Life Before Social Security"; Nancy J. Altman, *The Battle for Social Security*, New York: John Wiley and Sons, 2005, p.7.
5   Patricia P. Martin and David A. Weaver, "Social Security: A Program and Policy History," *Social Security Bulletin*, Vol. 66, No. 1, 2005; Peter J. Ferrara and Michael Tanner, "A New Deal for Social Security," pp. 13-18.
6   Frances Perkins, "The Roots of Social Security," Speech delivered at the headquarters of the Social Security Administration, 1962, http://www.ssa.gov/history/perkins5.html.
7   Frances Perkins, "The Roots of Social Security."
8   Ferrera and Tanner, p. 19.

Frances Perkins and the Spiritual Foundation of the New Deal by Donn Mitchell

This essay was adapted from a lecture for the Frances Perkins Day Observance at St. Andrew's Church, Newcastle, Maine, May 16, 2010.

1   Vida Dutton Scudder, *Father Huntington*, New York: E.P. Dutton & Co., Inc., 1940, p. 162.
2   Stanley P. Chyet, "The Political Rights of the Jews in the United States, 1776-1840," *Critical Studies in American Jewish History,* Vol. 2, New York: Ktav Publishing House, Inc., 1958, pp. 44-45.
3   Gregory Baum, *Catholics and Canadian Socialism: Political Thought in the Thirties and Forties*, New York: Paulist Press, 1980, p. 45.
4   George Martin, *Madam Secretary*, Boston: Houghton Mifflin Company, 1976.
5   Parish records at the Church of the Holy Spirit, Lake Forest, and St. Clement's, Philadelphia, do not establish a transfer of membership; however, occasional references to St. Clement's appear in Perkins's correspondence.
6   James E. Lindsley, *This Planted Vine*, New York: Harper & Row, 1984, p. 266, 285.
7   *Episcopalians at Work in the World*, New York: National Council of the Episcopal Church, 1949, p. 56.
8   Martin, *Madam Secretary*, p. 238.
9   This is the author's paraphrase.

FRANCES PERKINS AND THE ADMINISTRATION OF SOCIAL SECURITY
BY LARRY DEWITT

1   Altmeyer 1966, 36-37.
2   Perkins, 1946, 301.
3   Letter dated February 25, 1935, from France Perkins to President Roosevelt. FDR Presidential Library & Museum (item on display in Social Security exhibit).
4   Perkins, 1946, 301.
5   Arthur Krock, "Adjournment Plans Fail," *The New York Times*, August 25, 1935, pg. 1.
6   Film of Long speech, Universal Newsreel Broadcast, 1935.
7   Frances Perkins, "The Roots of Social Security," speech delivered at the Social Security Administration in Baltimore, Maryland, October 23, 1962. Text available online at: http://www.ssa.gov/history/perkins5.html
8   Frances Perkins, "The Roots of Social Security."
9   Frances Perkins, speech on the occasion of the 25th anniversary of the Social Security Act, August 15, 1960. Text available online at: http://www.ssa.gov/history/perkins6.html

A FIERCE DETERMINATION TO IMPROVE: SOCIAL SECURITY AND IBM
BY PAUL LASEWICZ

1   25th Anniversary Celebration of the Signing of the Social Security Act Department of Health, Education, and Welfare August 15, 1960 Social Security Online/History/Speeches and Articles/Frances Perkins retrieved November 24, 2009 http://www.ssa.gov/history/perkins6.html
2   Elwood J. Way Oral History, October 29, 1973, conducted by Dr. Abe Bortz, SSA Archives
3   Elwood J. Way Oral History, October 29, 1973, conducted by Dr. Abe Bortz, SSA Archives; History of DAO, James J. 'Obie' O'Beirne, Fall, 1961, SSA Archives
4   Elwood J. Way Oral History, October 29, 1973, conducted by Dr. Abe Bortz, SSA Archives
5   *Business Machines*, Feb. 10, 1934, vol. 16, no. 8, p. 17
6   Elwood J. Way Oral History, October 29, 1973, conducted by Dr. Abe Bortz, SSA Archives
7   Elwood J. Way Oral History, October 29, 1973, conducted by Dr. Abe Bortz, SSA Archives
8   Elwood J. Way Oral History, October 29, 1973, conducted by Dr. Abe Bortz, SSA Archives
9   History of DAO, James J. 'Obie' O'Beirne, Fall, 1961, SSA Archives
10 Elwood J. Way Oral History, October 29, 1973, conducted by Dr. Abe Bortz, SSA Archives
11 Elwood J. Way Oral History, October 29, 1973, conducted by Dr. Abe Bortz, SSA Archives
12 Murray Latimer Oral History, April 10, 1973, conducted by Dr. Abe Bortz, SSA Archives
13 History of DAO, James J. 'Obie' O'Beirne, Fall, 1961, SSA Archives
14 Charles McKinley, Robert W. Frase, Launching Social Security, University of Wisconsin Press, Madison WI, 1970, p. 20-21.
15 History of DAO, James J. 'Obie' O'Beirne, Fall, 1961, SSA Archives; anonymous, "History of Division of Accounting Operations" SSA Archives Folder: Systems - History
16 Elwood J. Way Oral History, October 29, 1973, conducted by Dr. Abe Bortz, SSA Archives; Mulliner on Winant; Maurine Mulliner Oral History, March 29, 1966, conducted by Dr. Abe Bortz, SSA Archives
17 Jack S. Futterman Oral History, July 16, 1996, conducted by Larry DeWitt, SSA Archives
18 Elwood J. Way Oral History, October 29, 1973, conducted by Dr. Abe Bortz, SSA Archives
19 H.J. McDonald, Oral History, August 1969, Reference File #154: Social Security
20 Report prepared for Watson Sr. biography, 1957 – RG11: Watson Sr./Personal/Belden Materials/IBM's First Social Security Contract B1054, F5

21 Appendix E August 19, 1936 meeting minutes memorandum (dated August 21), Systems –
    Proposals From Companies for Equipment, SSA Archives
22 Appendix E – August 25, 1936 meeting minutes memorandum, Systems – Proposals From
    Companies for Equipment, SSA Archives
23 25th Anniversary Celebration of the Signing of the Social Security Act Department of
    Health, Education, and Welfare August 15, 1960 Social Security Online/History/Speeches
    and Articles/Frances Perkins retrieved November 24, 2009 http://www.ssa.gov/history/
    perkins6.html
24 History of DAO, James J. 'Obie' O'Beirne, Fall, 1961, SSA Archives
25 *Business Machines,* June 18, 1936
26 Elwood J. Way Oral History, October 29, 1973, conducted by Dr. Abe Bortz, SSA Archives
27 Elwood J. Way Oral History, October 29, 1973, conducted by Dr. Abe Bortz, SSA Archives
28 Elwood J. Way Oral History, October 29, 1973, conducted by Dr. Abe Bortz, SSA Archives
29 History of DAO, James J. 'Obie' O'Beirne, Fall, 1961, SSA Archives
30 "You Can Go Home Again", OASIS March, 1982, p.19
31 Jack S. Futterman Oral History, July 16, 1996, conducted by Larry DeWitt, SSA Archives
32 French, Frances, "Down By The Waterfront", OASIS October 1976, p.19ff.; Wentzel, Michael,
    "Bits of Baltimore", The Evening Sun, November 12, 1979, p. B1
33 Bane, Frank, "Getting FDR's Help In Finding A Home", OASIS June 1977, p. 22
34 History of DAO, James J. 'Obie' O'Beirne, Fall, 1961, SSA Archives; Charles McKinley, Robert
    W. Frase, Launching Social Security, University of Wisconsin Press, Madison WI, 1970, p. 375.
35 Elwood J. Way Oral History, October 29, 1973, conducted by Dr. Abe Bortz, SSA Archives
36 Elwood J. Way Oral History, October 29, 1973, conducted by Dr. Abe Bortz, SSA Archives
37 "Tabulating Begun On Pension Forms", Baltimore Sun, December 2, 1936, SSA Archives;
    "1000 More Helpers Wanted at Once by Security Board", Washington News, December 5, 1936
    SSA Archives; IBM Business Machines, April 8, 1937
38 History of DAO, James J. 'Obie' O'Beirne, Fall, 1961, SSA Archives
39 October 16, 1937 RG11: Watson Sr./IBM Domestic – Government/US – Social Security Board,
    1937-1946 B614 F6
40 Meeting Minutes September 30, 1936 Reference File #154: Social Security, IBM Archives
41 *Business Machines,* March 11, 1937
42 IBM Record, July 3, 1953, Vol. 36, Issue 14, p. 3; Louis LaMotte was the brother of Robert
    LaMotte. Red took over IBM's Federal Account in early 1937, and later became an IBM
    executive vice president and director of the company.
43 Jack S. Futterman Oral History, July 16, 1996, conducted by Larry DeWitt, SSA Archives

THE IMPACT OF SOCIAL SECURITY ON AMERICAN LIVES BY NANCY J. ALTMAN

Parts of this article also appear in the author's book, The Battle for Social Security: From FDR's
Vision to Bush's Gamble, *Hoboken: John Wiley & Sons, Inc., 2005.*

1 E. T. Devine, Misery and Its Causes, p. 125, quoted in Abraham Epstein, Facing Old Age, New
   York: Alfred A. Knopf 1922, p.4
2 Report of the Committee on Economic Security, "The Economic Problems of Old Age," Part
   II, Old-Age Security, U.S. Social Security in America, Washington: U.S. Government Printing
   Office, 1937, p. 138, at http://www.ssa.gov/history/reports/ces/cesbookc7.html
3 "Old Age Security Staff Report to Mr. Witte," Volume II: Final Staff Report, Old Age Security,
   Committee on Economic Security (January, 1935), at http://www.ssa.gov/history/reports/
   ces/ces2armstaff.html.

4   Arloc Sherman and Isaac Shapiro, "Social Security Lifts 13 Million Seniors Above the Poverty Line," Center on Budget and Policy Priorities, February 24, 2005, at http://www.cbpp.org/2-24-05socsec.htm.

5   Roosevelt, Annual Message to the Legislature, 1931, in Joseph P. Harris, Brief in Defense of Old-Age Benefits as provided in the Social Security Bill, Papers in Support of Old-Age Provisions of Bill, Volume II: Old Age Security. U.S. Social Security Board, Social Security in America (Washington, DC: U.S. Government Printing Office, 1937), available at http://www.ssa.gov/history/reports/ces/ces2harrisbrief.html.

6   Fireside Chat 5 (June 28, 1934) On the Seventy-third Congress, Speeches, Franklin D. Roosevelt, Miller Center of Public Affairs, University of Virginia, at http://www.millercenter.virginia.edu/scripps/digitalarchive/speeches/spe_1934_0628_roosevelt.

7   L. W. Squier, "Old Age Dependency in the United States," pp. 28-9, in Abraham Epstein, *Facing Old Age*, New York: Alfred A. Knopf 1922, p. 21.

FRAMING SOCIAL SECURITY FOR THE TWENTY-FIRST CENTURY
BY ERIC R. KINGSON

References used in this essay:

Altman, Nancy J. (2005). *The Battle for Social Security: From FDR's Vision to Bush's Gamble.* Hoboken, New Jersey: John Wiley and Sons.

Altman, Nancy J. and Eric R. Kingson (2010, November 1). "Protect and Defend Social Security, Even While Reducing the Deficit." In *Spotlight on Poverty and Opportunity,* "Poverty, Opportunity, and the Deficit: Notes for the President's Commission" http://www.spotlightonpoverty.org/news.aspx?id=d1b26ba7-fabd-4dac-8fde-d3bb62b0edf4.

Ball, Robert M. (1998). *Straight talk about Social Security: An analysis of the issues in the current debate.* New York, New York: The Century Foundation Press.

Berkowitz, Edward D. (1997). The Historical Development of Social Security in the United States. In E.R. Kingson & J.H. Schulz, editors (1997). *Social Security in the 21st Century.* New York: Oxford University Press.

Brown, J. Douglas (1977). *Essays on Social Security.* Princeton, New Jersey: Princeton University Press.

Butler, S., & Germanis, P. (1983). Achieving a 'Leninist' strategy." *Cato Journal,* 3(2).

Derthick, M. 1979. *Policy Making for Social Security.* Washington, D.C.: The Brookings Institution.

Diamond, Peter A., and Orszag, Peter R. 2005. *Saving Social Security: A Balanced Approach.* Washington, DC: Brookings Institution Press.

Hohaus, R. A. (1960). Equity, Adequacy and Related Factors in Old Age Security. In W. Haber and W. J. Cohen (Eds.), *Social Security Programs, Problems and Policies.* Homewood, Illinois: Richard D. Irwin, Inc.

Kingson, E.R. (1984, September). Financing Social Security: Agenda-setting and the enactment of the 1983 amendments to the Social Security Act. *Policy Studies Journal.*

Kingson, E.R. J.M. Cornman & A.L. Torre-Norton (2009). The future of Social Insurance: Values and Generational Interdependence. In C. Estes and L. Rogne (editors), *Social Insurance, Social Justice, and Social Change* (Springer Publishers).

Kingson, E. R., & Williamson, J. B. (1993). The generational equity debate: A progressive framing of a conservative issue. *The Journal of Aging and Social Policy,* 5(3), 31–53.

Lamm, R. (1985). *Mega-traumas: America at the Year 200.* Boston, MA: Houghton Mifflin Company.

Light, Paul (1995). Still Artful Work: The Continuing Politics of Social Security Reform (New York, N.Y.: McGraw Hill.

Perkins, Francis (1934). People at Work. New York, N.Y.: The John Day Company.

Peterson, P. G., & Howe, N. (2004). On borrowed time: How the growth in entitlement spending threatens America's Future. Somerset, N.J.: Transaction Publishers

Quadagno, J. (1996). Social Security and the myth of the entitlement "crisis." *The Gerontologist,* 36(3).

Roosevelt, Franklin D. (1934, June 8). Message to Congress on the Objectives and Accomplishments of the Administration, June 8, 1934 www.presidency.ucsb.edu/ws/index. php?pd=14690

Schulz, James H. and Robert H. Binstock (2006). *Aging Nation: The Economics and Politics of Growing Older in America.* Westport, CT: Praeger Publishers.

Social Security Administration (1979). Labor Under the New Deal and the New Frontier. Baltimore, Maryland: Social Security Administration.

Steuerle, C.Eugene and Jon M. Bakija (1994). *Retooling Social Security for the Twenty-First Century.* Washington, D.C.: Urban Institute Press.

Toner, R. (1995). Word for word / Advice for Republicans; Attention! All sales reps for the contract with America! *The New York Times* (February 5).

Wallis, Jim (2010). Rediscovering Values: On Wall Street, Main Street, and Your Street. New York, NY: Howard Books.

White, Joseph (2001). *False Alarm.* New York, New York: The Century Foundation Press.